Dave Kahle's

INSIGHTS & ANSWERS

*Real life solutions to help distributor salespeople survive
and thrive in a changing economic environment*

Dave Kahle's

INSIGHTS & ANSWERS

*Real life solutions to help distributor salespeople survive
and thrive in a changing economic environment*

Published by
The DaCo Corporation
P.O. Box 230017
Grand Rapids, Michigan 49523

Dave Kahle's

INSIGHTS & ANSWERS

ISBN 0-9729289-1-X

The DaCo Corporation
PO BOX 230017 • GRAND RAPIDS, MI 49523
1.800.331.1287 • FAX: 616.451.9412
www.davekahle.com

TABLE OF CONTENTS

FOREWORD

It's more difficult to be an effective, professional distributor salesperson today than at any time in the past. That means that the committed professional salesperson needs access to all the resources he can get his hands on to help him do his job effectively.

It's for that reason that I decided to compile this set of material. As a 30+ year veteran of the sales wars, I've often observed that there is a huge gap between the theory of how to do your job well, and the practical day-to-day reality of the job. I've made it my mission to step into that gap with fundamentally sound, easy to understand, easy to implement, practical ideas for the field salesperson.

This book continues that tradition. You'll find articles and Questions and Answers from my Ezine, "*Thinking About Sales*." All of this material is designed to be used by the committed distributor salesperson (or his/her boss) to provide guidance in specific areas of the job.

I've provided a baker's dozen articles on topics that are of high concern to most distributors. Following each article is a selection of Q&As from my Ezine – these are questions asked by salespeople and my replies. Each set of Q&As relates to the article that they follow, expanding on the ideas expressed. Together, the article and the associated Q&As provide some unique and useful insights on the issues that are of most importance to salespeople.

You will find this material helpful in two ways: First, you may want to read through the book from cover to cover. It will give you insights on some of the most pressing issues you face.

Or, you may want to pick and choose the topics that are most urgent to you, allowing your day-to-day activities to dictate the order in which you review the material.

You will find the material to be helpful to you regardless of the method you choose to engage with it.

It is my hope that the material will equip you to, *"Go forth and sell well."*

Dave Kahle's

INSIGHTS & ANSWERS

*Real life solutions to help distributor salespeople survive
and thrive in a changing economic environment*

1

EVALUATING YOURSELF

The Five Most Common Mistakes Distributor Salespeople Make

Over the years that I've been involved in distribution, I've worked with tens of thousands of salespeople. Certain negative tendencies — mistakes that distributor salespeople make — keep surfacing. Here's my top five. See to what degree you (or your sales force) may be guilty of them.

Mistake Number One: Ruts! (Addiction to comfort zones.)

It is the unique nature of the distribution business that salespeople see the same customers over and over again. Regardless of how many accounts they have, whether 20 or 200, they see their customers much more frequently than almost any other type of salesperson. As a result, it's very easy to slide into the routine of seeing the same people at around the same time and talking about the same things.

Not only is it easy to get into ruts regarding which customers to see, it is also easy to extend that "stay in your comfort zones" mentality to the other aspects of the job. It becomes easy to stick to selling the same products, visiting the same departments and selling in the same way.

There was a time when the "same time next week" mode was a wise choice. Dependability was a desirable quality for a distributor salesperson. But, alas, the market has changed and most customers don't have time for the same conversation about fishing and football that they had last month.

But more insidious than this comfortable routine is the addiction to mental and emotional comfort zones. These comfort zones appear when a salesperson doesn't present that new product the company has just picked up – because the salesperson isn't comfortable with it. Or they evidence themselves when the salesperson refuses to learn the new computer system – because he or she isn't comfortable with that. Or when the salesperson doesn't call on a new market segment – just not comfortable.

> *The comfortable rut has become an almost insurmountable chasm, hindering the salesperson from reaching his/her potential.*

These are all evidences of a salesperson who is addicted to mental and emotional comfort zones. The comfortable rut has become an almost insurmountable chasm, hindering the salesperson from reaching his/her potential.

The problem is that as long as we remain within our comfort zones, we're destined to dwell in the past. We do what used to work, we sell what we have been comfortable with, we do our jobs the way we are used to doing them. We allow our past to determine our present and limit our future.

This may have been okay in years gone by, but the pace of change today won't reward the salesperson who is addicted to comfort zones built in previous days.

Personal and professional growth means continually venturing into unexplored areas, meeting new people, selling new products, and trying new methods, all with a mindset that understands the need for constant growth.

Mistake Number Two: Reactive Modality

It is so easy for salespeople to allow everyone else to dictate the course of their days. They carve out little empires of importance for themselves so they can constantly react and thereby be busy and feel needed. They train their customers to call them with routine questions when they could just as easily have called customer service. They need to be there to personally write down every order. They jump every time even the smallest customer calls. They must personally supervise every complex order, drop off every sample, and expedite every problem. Why? Because they want to feel important by being in such demand.

They aim to please, and they define that as reacting and responding to whatever comes their way. As a result, they develop for themselves days filled with frenzied activity. They drove this emergency shipment over to this customer, dropped off a sample to that one, checked on a couple of back orders for others, sourced some esoteric product for another. It's all so unnecessary. All this because they allowed and encouraged everyone else to dictate their activities. Where do they go tomorrow? Depends on who calls today. Instead of developing plans and working proactively, they let everyone else determine their days, and work reactively.

The net result? They squander their talents, time, energy and wisdom in a random distribution dictated by everyone else in the world. At the end of the day, they are exhausted. They are crabby to their spouses, irritable with their families, and negative about their companies and their jobs.

3

Mistake Number Three: Wasting the Sales Interaction By Not Learning More About the Customer.

There are some customers who have been called on for years, and yet the salesperson doesn't know any more about them today than he/she did after the second sales call. These are accounts where the salesperson cannot identify one of the account's customers, explain whether or not they are profitable, or identify one of their strategic goals.

> *There are some customers who have been called on for years, and yet the salesperson doesn't know any more about them today than he/she did after the second sales call.*

Distributor salespeople have this wonderful opportunity to learn about their customers in deeper and more detailed ways, and often squander it by having the same conversations with the same customers over and over. They never dig deeper. They mistake familiarity with knowledge.

What a shame. I am convinced that the ultimate sales skill — the one portion of the sales process that more than anything else determines our success as a salesperson — is the ability to know the customer deeper and in a more detailed way than our competitors do.

It's our knowledge of the customer that allows us to position ourselves as competent, trustworthy consultants. It's our knowledge of the customer that provides us the information we need to structure programs and proposals that distinguish us from everyone else. It's our knowledge of the customer that allows us to proactively service that customer, to meet their needs even before they have articulated them.

In an economic environment where the distinctions between companies and products are blurring in the eyes of the customer, the successful companies and individuals will be those who outsell the rest. And outselling the rest depends on understanding the customer better than anyone else.

Mistake Number Four: Poor Questioning

This is a variation of the mistake above. I am absolutely astonished at the lack of thoughtfulness that I often see on the part of distributor salespeople. Most use questions like sledgehammers, splintering the relationship and bruising the sensibility of their customers by thoughtless questions.

Others don't use them at all, practically ignoring the most important part of a sales call. They labor under the misconception that the more they talk, the better job of selling they do, when the truth lies in exactly the opposite direction.

> *They labor under the misconception that the more they talk, the better job of selling they do, when the truth lies in exactly the opposite direction.*

And others are content to play about the surface of the issue. "How much of this do you use?" "What do you not like about your current supplier?" Their questions are superficial at best, redundant and irritating at worst.

The result? Salespeople never really uncover the deeper more intense issues that motivate their customers. Instead, they continually react to the common complaint of customers who have been given no reason to think otherwise: "Your price is too high."

Fewer sales, constant complaints about pricing, frustrated salespeople, impatient managers, and unimpressed customers – all of these as a result of the inability to use the salesperson's most powerful tool with skill and sensitivity.

Mistake Number Five: No Investment in Themselves.

Here's an amazing observation. No more than 5% to 10% of active, full time professional distributor salespeople ever invest in their own growth. That means that only one of 20 salespeople have ever spent $20.00 of their own money on a book on sales, or subscribed to a sales magazine, taken a sales course, or attended a sales seminar of their own choosing and on their own nickel.

> *Distributor sales is the only profession I know of where the overwhelming majority of practitioners are content with their personal status quo.*

Don't believe me? Take a poll. Ask your salespeople or your colleagues how many of them have invested more than $20.00 in a book, magazine, tape, etc., in the last 12 months. Ask those who venture a positive answer to substantiate it by naming their investment. Don't be surprised if the answers get vague. You'll quickly find out how many salespeople in your organization have invested in themselves.

Distributor sales is the only profession I know of where the overwhelming majority of practitioners are content with their personal status quo.

Why is that? A number of reasons.

Some mistakenly think that their jobs are so unique that they cannot possibly learn anything from anyone else.

Still others think they know it all. They have, therefore, no interest in taking time from some seemingly valuable thing they are doing to attend a seminar or read a book.

Some don't care. Their focus is hanging onto their jobs, not necessarily getting better at them.

But I think the major reason is that the overwhelming majority of distributor salespeople do not view themselves as professionals and, therefore, do not have professional expectations for themselves. They worked their way up from the customer service desk or the warehouse, and they view their work as a job to be done, not a profession within which to grow.

They are content to let their companies arrange for their training or development. And between you and me, they would prefer that their companies really didn't do anything that would require them to actually change what they do.

These are the most common negative tendencies that I see. It may be that you and your colleagues are immune to these dampers on success. Good for you. But if you are not immune, and if you spot some of your own tendencies in this list, then you are not reaching your potential for success. You have tremendous potential for success — for contentment, confidence and competence – that is being hindered by these negative behaviors. Rid yourself of these negative tendencies, and you'll begin to reach your potential.

Five Most Common Negative Tendencies
of Distributor Salespeople

Self-Assessment

Use this self-test to determine the degree to which you (or your sales force) may be guilty of Dave's five biggest mistakes.

Directions: Circle all the statements that describe your behavior.

A. Comfort zones

1. You almost always visit the same people at about the same time.

2. When you have been tempted to call on a job title that may be new to you (like calling on the CFO and not just the purchasing agent) you found a reason not to do it.

3. The last time your company presented a new line or new product to you, you did not show it as much as your boss would have liked.

4. You were very slow to implement the last major change that the boss asked you to make – or you resisted making that change.

B. Reactive modality

5. You often spend a major portion of your day doing things that you had not planned to do that day.

6. You go into the office several days a week.

7. You have your customers call you for things that customer service or inside sales could do instead of you.

8. You personally expedite back orders, or source products for your customers that someone else in your company could have done.

C. Not learning about the customer

9. You don't use an account profile form, either electronic or paper.

10. You find yourself having the same conversation with the same people, month after month.

11. You would be hard pressed to identify one or two of your customer's customers.

12. You don't know most of the key decision makers in most of your good accounts.

D. Questioning

13. In most of your sales calls, you do most of the talking.

14. You don't know the goals and objectives your major customers have for their business.

15. You rarely prepare a question before the sales call.

16. You hear "your price is too high" almost all the time.

E. Personal Growth

17. You haven't spent more than $20.00 on improving your sales skills in the last 12 months.

18. You don't regularly listen to audio recordings, or read sales magazines, e-zines or newsletters.

19. You haven't been to a seminar to help improve your sales skills (product presentations by manufacturers don't count) in the last 12 months.

20. You think you pretty much know everything there is to know about selling in your job.

Scoring: Look at each of the five tendencies. If you circled more than two of the four items within that tendency, you are definitely guilty of it, and need to take intense corrective action. If you circled one of the behaviors, then you should watch this behavior of yours, and try to fine tune it. If you did not circle any within any of the tendencies, congratulations, you are probably not guilty of that negative tendency.

Q #1. Dave, on several occasions you have said that our customers want us to understand their business. How do we do that when we call on lots of different types of businesses? How do we become experts in everything?

A. Unless you are a real genius, you don't. Rather, you do two things:

1. You prioritize your prospects and customers, focusing your best efforts on a smaller number of customers who you decide are the highest potential customers. So, you decide that while you cannot become an expert on every customer, you can become an expert on a few. This requires you to "demote" some customers so that you can "promote" others. Choose those others well. See my video on "Prioritizing Your Customers." Or, read chapter two of my book, *10 Time Management Secrets for Salespeople*. Both of those explain in detail the concepts, processes and tools necessary to make cold-blooded business decisions about in which customers you should invest your valuable time.

2. Then, become adept at the processes and skills necessary to understand your customer better every time you meet with him/her. Regardless of what kind of business you are calling on, you can still drill deeper in that particular sales call, even if it's only one call a year. To do this, you focus on improving your observing, asking and listening skills.

So, you focus more precisely on a smaller number of high potential customers, and then you focus on using the time that you have to more completely understand every customer.

2

DEALING WITH CHANGE

The Ultimate Success Skill

These are incredibly difficult times for distributor salespeople.

Competition in almost every segment continues to intensify. At the same time, customers seem to expect more service and demand lower margins. Most markets are rapidly changing, and it's hard to keep up with the changes in technology and products.

Customers' demands seem to be a moving target. Sometimes it seems like the lowest price is all anyone is interested in, while at other times they talk about the need for trusting relationships and partnering with vendors.

These rapid changes are a mark of our times. In fact, the indications are that this rapid pace of change will continue unabated.

Consider this. In 1900, the total amount of knowledge that mankind had was doubling about every 500 years. In 1990, it was doubling about every two years. And the pace continues to increase. One futurist predicts that today's high school students will have to absorb more information in their senior year than their grandparents did in their entire life.

That incredibly rapid pace of new knowledge drives the forces of change at an unprecedented rate. It's almost as if a malevolent spirit were stalking our economy, rendering all the wisdom of the past useless, and casting a spell of confusion and uncertainty over the land.

As a consultant, I work with distributor executives and salespeople in a variety of industries. And almost invariably, during my first interview with a new client, I hear words something like this, "You need to understand that things are changing very rapidly in our industry."

I do understand, because I see things changing very rapidly in virtually every industry with which I work. And the indications are that this rapid state of change will not be a temporary phenomenon we all must live through. Rather, it will be the permanent condition we must accept for the foreseeable future.

Howard Stein said, "All I know is, things don't work like they used to work. So don't plan on doing anything based on the past."

But rapid change is only one of the forces that is surging through our culture and contributing to the uncertainty of our turbulent times.

Relentlessly Growing Complexity

In every direction we look, we see the world becoming more complex. On a world-wide basis, the evening news is dominated by reports of wars between countries we didn't even know existed a year or two ago. The Soviet Union was one entity a short time ago. Today it's incredibly more complex.

Closer to our own lives, we see our markets splintering into more and more fragments. Products, energized by the explosion in knowledge and new technologies, are becoming increasingly more complex. For example, can you imagine a piece of equipment today that doesn't have a computer somewhere in its innards?

The services we buy and sell are becoming more complex as computer capabilities are folded into services of all types, and providers respond to the market demand for personalized service. For example, a few years ago we had one number to call for our phone service. Today there are so many vendors of various phone services that we need to employ people just to deflect their incoming calls.

Unfortunately, the trend toward growing complexity in every area of our business also shows no signs of weakening.

The business environment in the near future, therefore, will continue to be characterized by rapid change and growing complexity.

All this means that the skills, strategies, and tactics that have served you well in the past may be becoming obsolete. But here's an even more sobering thought – because of the rapid rate of change, the new skills and tactics that you develop today may well be obsolete in just a few years.

That means that in order to deal with these difficult times, salespeople need to be able to continually change what they are doing. They need to absorb new information created by our changing world, review their tactics in light of it, and change their behavior in positive ways.

> *Self-directed learning is the ability, on the part of the individual, to absorb new infor-mation about the world, and to change one's behavior in positive ways in response to it.*

In other words, they need to continually learn. The ultimate self-improvement skill in the 21st Century is the ability to master "self-directed learning."

When most of us hear the word "learning" we often associate it with formal school, or perhaps seminars and company-sponsored training programs. While these are all means of facilitating learning, they don't capture the essence of the ultimate self-improvement skill.

Self-directed learning is the ability, on the part of the individual, to absorb new information about the world, and to change one's behavior in positive ways in response to it. The key is behavior change. Learning without action is impotent. Knowledge that doesn't result in changed action is of little value.

Constant change in your behavior is the only reasonable response to a constantly changing world. Self-directed learning differs from the traditional approaches to "training" in that it requires the individual to assume complete responsibility for his own behavior change. The stimulus for the learning must come from the individual, and he/she must develop his own learning program to expose himself to new information, and to change his/her behavior appropriately.

Let's look at two fundamental areas of a salesperson's job in order to see how the need to "learn" is critical.

Products

The explosion in information has lead to technological innovation and change at a dizzying rate. This means that new products are coming into the market – every market – more quickly and more regularly than ever before.

The competent salesperson can no longer be content with his/her product knowledge. The product that is today's hot new seller will likely become an obsolete dinosaur within a couple of years.

> *The key is behavior change. Learning without action is impotent. Knowledge that doesn't result in changed action is of little value.*

So, salespeople must acquire the skills of constantly learning about new products and new technologies. There will be a continuous string of new language to learn, new features to understand, and new applications for new needs on the part of their customers. How long ago was it that none of us knew what a "Pentium" was, or what to do with a "DVD?"

Markets

On the other side of the selling equation, the markets – our customers – are changing just as rapidly. On one hand, there is a great deal of change in the names and styles of the players (Wal-Mart instead of thousands of independent businesses), while on the other, every industry is becoming more complex as the trend toward specialization creates a kaleidoscope of market segments in place of the homogeneous markets with which many of us grew up.

Salespeople will have to continually refine their interactive skills and deal with each customer as a unique individual. That will require them to learn more intently about their customers and the processes which are most effective with them – a never-ending challenge.

At the same time the world is changing rapidly for us, it is changing just as rapidly for our customers. One day it seems that the lowest price is the only concern. While the next day they talk about long-term "partnering" with trusted suppliers.

The competent salesperson not only has to keep up with changing customers, but also customers who change in their needs and demands.

Preparing to Master Self-Directed Learning

Proficiency at the ultimate self-improvement skill demands some new competencies from salespeople. While the specific skills are too detailed for this article, we can describe some of the qualities needed to enable a person to become an active self-directed learner.

> *Salespeople must accept the responsibility for their own behavior and for the consequence of that behavior.*

First, they must have an attitude of "pro-active" responsibility for their situation. In other words, they must believe that their actions have consequences, and that in order to change the consequences they must change their actions. This sounds so fundamental as to be ludicrous, yet it seems to be a concept that is foreign to much of the population. In recent years our culture has fostered a "blame someone else" attitude. Unfortunately, as long as we remain a victim of someone else, we have no responsibility to change our own behavior.

Salespeople must accept the responsibility for their own behavior and for the consequence of that behavior. As one of my clients said to me, "If you always do what you always did, you'll always get what you always got." Therefore, the need to change what you do, if you expect different consequences.

Next, salespeople engaging in self-directed learning need to have an openness to new information. Probably one of the sure harbingers of pending failure is the attitude that you know it all. Salespeople who will continue to improve themselves understand that they don't ever have all the answers. There is always something new to learn. And, like magnets, they're continually searching for new ideas, new perspectives, and new information to absorb.

And finally, they need to be able to follow through on their plans. They must have the ability to act on decisions they have made, and become creatures whose actions arise out of conscious thought rather than unconscious habit.

Given this set of attitudes, a salesperson can begin to master the procedures and disciplines that will characterize him/her as a "self-directed learner" and equip him to be successful in our turbulent times.

Chapter Two ~ Dealing with Change

Q #2. I've read your ideas about the need to invest in developing myself. Can you quantify that? How much time and money should I spend on my own education?

A. Now that's a question I'm rarely asked. It's refreshing to receive it.

I'm assuming that you are referring to your education beyond formal schooling. After you've finished your degree and you're done with your academic education, how much should you invest in your continual growth and development?

Let me share some research with you. ASTD, the association for training and development, does an annual survey of its member companies. While the numbers vary a little bit from year to year, generally good companies spend about 3 to 3.5% of payroll on training their employees. The Distribution Research and Education Foundation found that high performing distributors spend 2.5 % of payroll on training, while average distributors spend 1.3 %.

So, if you are asking from the perspective of your company, figure somewhere around 3% of your sales payroll will put you in the general area. In other words, if you have five salespeople, averaging $50,000 each, that's $250,000 in sales payroll. Three percent of that would be $7,500 spent each year in continuous development.

If you are asking from a personal perspective, the answer lies in how serious you are about developing yourself. A good way to gauge this is by using the same measurement – percent of payroll. In this case, the question is percent of your income. Let's say you make $50,000 a year. If you attend one of my sales Boot Camps, for example, you'll spend $1295 for tuition, plus the cost of the hotel and transportation. Let's figure about $1700, or a little over 3% of your gross income.

I believe that a serious salesperson, dedicated to making a career of professional sales and committed to improving himself, should be spending around 3 - 4% of income a year on the task.

What about investment of time? I believe a company ought to spend about four hours a month in developing its sales force. And the same for you, one hour a week, week in and week out.

Let's put this in perspective. Only about 5% of the salespeople in the world spent more than $20.00 on improving themselves in the last year. If you invest 3% of your income and one hour a week to continuous improvement, you'll soon rise in the ranks, as your competitors are generally content to stay where they are, investing minimally in their own development.

Q #3. I'm one of those salespeople who hasn't spent $20.00 this year on a book or seminar to improve myself. I just don't want to go to the trouble. I believe that I can learn sufficiently on the job, and I'm tired of going to school. Should I feel bad?

A. Now that's an honest question. Should you feel bad? My knee jerk reaction is to say, "of course." But, on further reflection, it depends on your approach to your job, and on your aspirations for yourself. First, a definition – "mastery." You achieve "mastery" of any profession when you are in the top 5% of performers in that profession. Pursuit of mastery is the process of continually striving to achieve and then to remain in the top 5% of your profession.

I believe that every serious professional salesperson ought to strive for mastery. If that applies to you, then you want to become as good as you can become. If you want the greater sense of fulfillment, the greater degree of respect, and the increase in economic status that mastery brings, then, yes, you should feel bad because you are not acting consistently with your aspiration.

So, from one perspective, I have to say yes, you should feel bad. But it is not an ideal world. And, realistically, only about 20% of salespeople have such aspirations. Most are content with the status quo. Most just want to do their job, go home at the end of the day, and be done with it. If that's you, then I guess you are living a life consistent with your values, and that's okay.

The difference is what you want for yourself and your family. If you are perfectly content with your situation and your results, if you do not want anything that can be achieved by higher performance, if you don't want to become something better than you are, then you are perfectly content, and contentment is the enemy of growth. If you want to be or achieve something that you are not now, that discontentment should lead you to the realization that you must change if you are going to achieve something more. And that realization should stimulate you to invest more heavily in your own development.

So, which are you ? Content with your situation, or discontent? The answer to "should you feel bad" depends on your position.

Q #4. *Dave, I'm interested in what you would recommend for a subscription to a monthly sales magazine and a sales improvement seminar.*

A. You have touched one of my hot-buttons with this question. So, forgive me if you get a longer answer than you expected.

First, let me applaud you for asking the question. As amazing as it sounds, I have come to the conclusion that only about 5% of salespeople ever invest in their own growth and improvement. My understanding of that number has evolved over the years. I used to think it was much higher, but the more experience I gain, the more I'm convinced that it's a rare and unusual salesperson who will actually spend $20.00 or so to improve himself/herself, much less to actually go to a seminar. So, just by asking the question, you have indicated that you are probably in that top percentile of salespeople. And, the fact that you probably will invest in improving yourself means that, over time, you will distance yourself from the pack.

Before I tackle your question head on, let me sketch a little more background. Here's a word to remember: *Learning event.* What's a learning event? It's an experience you have in which you encounter some new ideas, you gain insights in new ways of seeing existing ideas, or you are reminded of behaviors and practices of which you may have been aware, but from which you have gotten away.

So, reading a newsletter could be a learning event. So could a sales meeting or a conversation with one of your colleagues. So could five minutes spent after a sales call reflecting on what went well and what didn't.

What is important is this? As a result of a learning event, you focus on some better behavior that you are going to implement in the future. Learning, for adults, is all about behavior. In other words, you must find something that you can do differently, and decide to do that thing.

For example, you may have participated in one of my phone seminars. That's a learning event. Following the seminar, you say to yourself, "I really should spend more time prioritizing my customers, so that I don't waste my time with low potential accounts." That thought is the "better behavior" that you decided to pursue as a result of the learning event.

Generating those kinds of commitments is what learning is all about. When you asked for a recommendation, my belief is that you ultimately want to generate those commitments to "better behavior" in yourself or in the salespeople you manage.

I sometimes hear this kind of comment, "I knew that." This from an experienced salesperson following a seminar. My response is, "So what?" This is not about what you know, it's about what you do. So the question should not be, "Is this something new that you didn't know?" The question should be, "Is this something good that you are not doing, or that you could do better than you are now?"

The emphasis has to be on action (behavior), not just knowledge. Here's a real life example. I just now had a conversation with a sales manager calling me with a problem. He had read my "How to Excel at Distributor Sales" book, and was impressed with, among other things, the chapters on getting organized. He said, "It is such basic information, but yet they don't do it." He went on to say that getting your file system organized was fundamental, but when he rode with his salespeople, none of them had done it.

That's the point. They probably all knew that they should be organized. But none of them were doing it. You see, it wasn't about knowledge, it was about behavior.

If you want to continually improve, then you regularly answer the question: "What could I do better than I am now?" The question is not, "What do I not know that I should know?" It's not just knowledge, it's *knowledge applied* that is the issue.

The way you find answers to that question is to regularly engage in learning events.

In other words, rather than just one intense day-long seminar once a year, I'd prefer you to be involved in a learning event at least once a month, if not weekly. My recommendation is four hours once a month. The systematic and regular involvement in learning events puts you in the mindset of continuous improvement, constantly stimulates you with new "better behaviors" and allows you the time to focus on one or two areas of improvement every month.

That's why, by the way, I do the phone seminars once a month, and our Up-A-Notch ™ video programs are designed to be done once a month.

One more little piece of background before I provide some specific resources for you.

We all understand that people learn best in different ways. One thing that is rarely acknowledged is that different media generally have a slightly different impact on our learning. For example, when we take in something strictly by ear, we have a tendency to believe it more and remember it less. That's why you can't remember last Sunday's sermon in church. It may have sounded good at the time, but you've lost the message in the few days since then. Taking something in by reading has the opposite impact: We are more critical of the information, but we retain it longer. It's not as believable, but is more memorable.

The best learning experiences, then, require you to listen, to read, and to do. In that way, you are far more likely to gain helpful answers to the question, "What could I be doing better than I am now?" By the way, that explains why my telephone seminars, in-person programs and multi-media programs are configured and structured the way they are structured. They are all designed to maximize your learning by appealing to a multiple number of senses.

That brings us to this conclusion: If you are going to do "continuous improvement" effectively, then you need to regularly expose yourself to a variety of learning events, focusing on the question, "What could I do better than I am now?" as a way of gaining value from every experience.

Here, then, are a variety of resources:

1. **Newsletters.** Start with my *"Thinking about Sales."* Then look at *"NAW - Smart Brief"* (www.smartbrief.com/NAW). There are a number of other electronic newsletters available, and you should consider each that looks appealing.

   In terms of paper newsletters, I'm on the editorial advisory board of *"The Competitive Edge"* and recommend that, of course. I personally like *"Sales & Marketing Excellence"* (www.eep.com to sign up.)

2. **Magazines.** *Personal Selling Power* has been a good quality publication. I also subscribe to *Sales & Marketing Management* Magazine, which focuses both on management and sales. There are industry-specific publications for almost every trade group imaginable. Rather than attempt to list them here, let me just encourage you to get on their subscription lists. Contact the national association of companies who do what you do, and find out what publications are available for your industry.

3. **Seminars.** I have to admit that I'm a terrible critic of others in my business. I think there is so much fluff passed off as information by people who have no idea how to help people learn, that it's outrageous. So, I rarely find someone to recommend.

   Of course you should be a regular or master subscriber to TGIF & K, my series of monthly telephone seminars. Look for my "Top Gun" seminars for distributors, as well as my "Time Management" seminars. I honestly think that my programs are the best in the world because I'm the only educator in the field of sales and growth that I know of who combines a deep understanding of how people learn best with a wealth of practical, street smart, real-world expertise.

   Beyond that, there are dozens of learning events in the form of seminars. Ask around, and get word-of-mouth recommendations from people whose opinion you respect. AMA does a good job with almost everything they produce, although they are a little pricey.

4. **Books.** With about 50,000 books published in this country every year, you have an almost limitless variety from which to choose. I'm regularly asked to recommend a good book. My response is this: Read my books first. After you have read my books, then it really doesn't matter much. If your attitude is right and you prepare your mind with the question, "What could I do better than I am now?, you'll find something of value from almost any book.

   Go to the library or the local book store, and pick up whatever appeals to you that day. Having said that, I have to admit that I am impressed with Neil Rackham's books, and recommend them highly.

5. **Other resources.** Self-study, multimedia programs are highly effective because they appeal to all the basic ways to learn. I specialized in them, and you'll find a variety on my website. If you really want to get serious, check our self-study sales certification program – but remember, it's only for the top five-percenters of the world.

   The jury is still out on web-based media as a learning media for soft-skills. There is no doubt that CBT (computer based training) can be effective for skills like learning a new piece of software, but it is yet unproven for things like learning to ask questions effectively, or handling objections. With that in mind, I like the www.youachieve.com web site and think that it has potential.

Whew! Now that's a long answer to a short question. Hope this helps.

3

INTEGRITY

Is Integrity a Sales Strategy?

I was speaking to a group of professional salespeople in Johannesburg, South Africa, on the subject of integrity in business. At dinner later in the evening, my host, who had been sitting in the audience, sheepishly shared with me that several of the people seated near her snickered at the idea. Evidently, to them sales was just a series of transactions, and the salesperson's job was to wring as much money out of each transaction as possible, under whatever means were necessary.

Their position was, I believe, both sad as well as unwise. I believe that there are certainly practices in the business world where morality perfectly coincides with wise business. Integrity is one such practice. It is both good business as well as good morals.

I believe it is such good business that salespeople should adhere to a no-exceptions policy of maintaining absolute integrity. I'm not going to make the case for absolute honesty as a moral policy. That's better left to our churches to do. There is, however, a powerful case to be made for honesty from a practical point of view.

31

Honesty is a powerful sales strategy that is probably more important today than ever before.

> *I believe that there are certainly practices in the business world where morality perfectly coincides with wise business. Integrity is one such practice. It is both good business as well as good morals.*

It works like this. If you have integrity, you save your customers time. In today's frenzied world, time is more precious than money for a lot of people. If your customers cannot believe you, then they must spend hours, days or weeks of precious time confirming the representations you have made. If, however, they can believe you, then they don't feel the need to check for the veracity of every fact or statement.

Here's an illustration. A few years ago, we attempted to purchase a condominium. The condo was in a resort location, and had been used as a rental unit. So, it came fully furnished, down to the silverware and cooking utensils. We thought it was a good value, a wise investment, and offered the owner exactly the price he was asking. Shortly thereafter, word came from the real estate agent that the owner, on receiving our full price offer, had increased his price.

The owner may have been looking at his action as a slick negotiating ploy. We saw it as a lack of integrity. If we couldn't believe his stated price, then we couldn't believe any of the representations he had made. We would be reduced to counting the number of knives and forks instead of believing the inventory sheet provided for us. We didn't want to waste the time checking out every aspect of the deal. If we couldn't trust some of the representations by the owner, then we couldn't trust any. And, if we couldn't trust any, it wasn't worth it to us to take the risk in dealing with him. We walked away from the deal.

We saw the owner's lack of integrity as causing us to invest a great deal of time to assure ourselves that the risk was worth the money. In this case, we were the buyers who saw the seller's lack of integrity as causing us to spend more time on the project. We chose not to do that.

The same is true of your customers. The more your customer trusts you, the less risk your customer feels in dealing with you, and the less time necessary to invest in understanding the product, service or program you are offering. From the customer's perspective, it's easier and less risky to deal with someone you trust than with someone you don't trust.

> *The more your customer trusts you, the less risk your customer feels in dealing with you, and the less time necessary to invest in understanding the product, service or program you are offering.*

And that can translate directly into dollars. I'm always willing to pay more for something if I can buy it with less risk. In other words, if I can buy it from a company or person I can trust. On the other hand, I'd rather not buy something at all if I have suspicious feelings about the vendor.

Here's another example. A few years ago I grew jealous of my neighbor's lawn. His was far greener, thicker and fuller than my lawn. It was because he had a lawn care service fertilize his lawn several times each year. I determined to do the same thing. So I obtained the name and phone number of the company he used, formed an idea of what the service would cost me, and decided to do business with that company.

I called the company, ready to buy the service. When I inquired about the types of service available, the salesperson indicated that there were several options available. Now, I'm a visually oriented person, and I like to make decisions based on what I read, not on what I hear. So, I said, "Okay, why not come out and do the first application, and then leave me a brochure so that I can review my options, and then I'll make a decision?" The salesperson agreed.

We then reviewed the details of my location, and the approximate date for the first fertilizer application. It was a deal. The salesperson then repeated our agreement, saying, "Okay, we'll be out to do the first application and we'll leave a brochure, and then you can cancel at any time with 30 days notice."

"What?" I said.

He repeated his comment. "Wait a minute," I said. "I only agreed to one application. I'm not committing to any ongoing contract until I check out all the options."

"But that's not how we do it," the salesperson stammered.

"No," I said.

"But, But..." more stammers.

"No," I said again. "Forget it. Cancel me."

What happened? Here I was, as good a prospect as there ever was. I was ready to purchase, having decided to use this company, even calling them to make the purchase. Yet something in what the salesperson said raised a red flag in my mind, and made me doubt the integrity of the person, and by inference, the company. He had originally said that I would be billed for only one application, and then implied that I was committing to an ongoing program.

I viewed that as being deceitful, or at best, manipulative. If I can't trust them on that, on what can I trust them? There are lots of other lawn care companies, and the next one in the yellow pages got my business. Life's too short, and business is too busy to deal with people you can't trust.

The question, then, for you as a salesperson is this: Do your customers see you as trustworthy?

That's a difficult question to answer. You can't just ask them, because you know you are unlikely to hear a candid response. But you can gain a sense of their perception of you by looking for some of the symptoms of trust or a lack of it.

For example, if you find your customers sometimes buying from a higher priced source, or buying a product or service you consider to be inferior, it may be that your customer doesn't trust you!

On the other hand, if you find your customers accepting your word, and choosing to deal with you, even when you are offering an identical product at a higher price, then chances are they do trust you. Your reputation for honesty and integrity has been a smart business strategy, resulting in measurable benefits to you.

Unfortunately, a reputation for trustworthiness and honesty is not a result of one event or a single transaction. It doesn't develop out of some clever phrases you memorize and repeat. Rather, it develops over time as you adhere to a set of ethical standards in small as well as big things. It's not a technique you use; rather it's the person you chose to become. As you strive to adhere to the standard of absolute honesty and integrity in all that you do, you'll develop a character trait that will become evident to everyone around you, including your customers. And that is good business as well as good morals.

Chapter Three ~ Integrity

Q #5. My company wants me to sell a product that I do not believe is ready. I don't believe it does what they claim it will do. I'm afraid that if I promote it, I'll lose the trust of my customers. Have you ever encountered a situation like this? Any recommendations?

A. I lived through almost exactly the same situation. In my case, the product was a medical device that didn't do what the company said it would do. Not only were we expected to sell it, we were given quotas and told that our jobs depended on our performance. It bordered on a threat.

So, to put it in perspective, I was being asked (more accurately I was being told) to do something that I felt was unethical. I suppose there are several things I could have done:

1. Refused to sell it, and let the company know exactly why, thus putting my job in jeopardy.

2. Sold it, knowing that I would be violating my customer's trust.

3. Said that I would sell it, but then give only half-hearted efforts so that I actually did not sell any.

4. Attempt to sell it, but share with my customer my reservations about the product.

5. Quit.

I believe that when you are faced with an ethical dilemma like this, in which your company is asking or directing you to do something which violates your ethical standards, these are your options. There may be others that arise out of the specifics of your situation, but certainly you have at least these five options.

The first step towards resolving this is to clearly identify your options. Now that you have done that, the real question is one that I can't answer for you. It has to do with how sensitive your conscience is, and to how refined your sense of ethics.

In my case, I decided that I could not do option number two, because I would be ruining my reputation. I believe that my reputation is, as Proverbs says: ***"A good name is more desirable than great riches; to be esteemed is better than silver or gold" (Proverbs 22:1)*** So, I decided option two was not for me.

I also ruled out option four. To do that would be to detract from my customer's faith and trust in my company. As a loyal employee, I didn't believe in that, either. I believe that I should do whatever I can to support and build up my company, even if I don't always agree with them. To share some of my concerns would be to make my company look bad, and I didn't want to do that.

Option three seemed like a wimpy option, and deceptive. So, I eliminated that. Which lead me to either selling it, confronting the company with my position, or quitting. I chose option one: To not sell it, and share my position with the company. I was fully aware of the possible consequences of my actions. Even though I loved the job, I was ready to leave it.

That's where the plot thickened. When I shared my position with my manager, he said words to the effect that he was leaving in the next month or two and that there would be several months without any manager in the territory. And by then, the whole issue would have been resolved. So, don't worry about it.

At that point, I decided that I had fulfilled my responsibility and had informed my manager of my position. What he did with it was his choice. I felt no need to belabor the point by going to his boss. So, I did what he told me to do. I didn't sell it. And I didn't worry about it. And the situation did resolve itself in a few months.

I'm not sure how instructive that is for you. Since that was the route that I took, it's the one that I advocate for you. However, I've been around enough to know that individual circumstances can make a big difference.

My ultimate advice is to make sure that your conscience is at ease with whatever you decide. Don't make a decision that will result in turmoil and sleepless nights.

Chapter Three ~ Integrity

Q # 6. What do you do with the person that implies they want something, i.e. gifts, to do business?

A. My personal philosophy is not to provide personal gifts for corporate business. That doesn't mean that I don't occasionally send a gift to one of my clients, but it is more in the form of "thanks for your continued business" than it is an incentive to do more business. There's a fine line between a gift and a bribe. I'd rather be well inside that line by walking away from any piece of business that I thought was tainted.

On the other hand, I understand that personal incentives are routine in some other countries. So, I think you need to get your manager's opinion and your company's policy on this. Then think through your own personal ethical position, and make a decision from there.

4

STRATEGIC PLANNING

Strategic Planning for Salespeople

"Ready, shoot, aim." Unfortunately, that's the all too common description of the distributor salesperson's modus operandi. In a misguided attempt to stay busy and see as many people as possible, too many salespeople subscribe to the theory that any activity is good activity.

There was a time when this was true. Customers had more time, sales was a simpler job, and any conversation with a prospect or customer was a good thing. But times have changed, and the job of the salesperson has become much more complex. The pressure on the salesperson to make good decisions about the effective use of his time has never been greater. Salespeople now must confront an overwhelming number of potential "things to do," and that requires them to make decisions about which customers in which to invest their time, to prioritize their activities every day, and to continually choose from a menu of possible activities. In other words, salespeople must now engage in strategic planning.

Not that this is new. There have always been salespeople who have regularly planned strategically for the effective use of their time. It's been a characteristic of superstar salespeople and highly effective sales forces. For that small percentage that do it instinctively, or are encouraged to do so by their management, it's as much a part of their routine as brushing their teeth in the morning.

Unfortunately, that describes the minority of salespeople and sales forces in the world. What was a practice of only the best has now become a requirement for everyone. Most salespeople have never been trained in the best practices, processes and disciplines that will set them apart from the pack. In this case, that means that most salespeople have never been exposed to the principles, processes and disciplines of effective strategic planning.

> *What was a practice of only the best has now become a requirement for everyone.*

Let's define our terms. A *strategic plan* is composed of a set of measurable goals, coupled with a list of the most important, most effective things you (or your company) can do to reach those goals. A strategic plan is not a detailed action plan. That comes later. The plan itself is often limited to no more than two or three pages. The idea is to identify the highest priority and most effective: too much detail defeats the purpose.

Strategic planning is the process of thinking about your job (or your company) in such a way so as to develop your strategic plan.

> *A strategic plan is composed of a set of measurable goals, coupled with a list of the most important, most effective things you (or your company) can do to reach those goals.*

Creating a strategic plan for your company always involves a dedicated chunk of time devoted to the process. So, too, for a strategic plan for a salesperson. Creating a strategic plan for your company always involves some preparation, and a gathering of the best minds in the company. So, too, for a salesperson's strategic plan: Preparation and a melding of the ideas of the salesperson and his/her manager. Strategic planning for your company always involves the discipline to adhere to a formalized process. So, too, for a salesperson.

With your company, the creation of a strategic plan is often an energizing, inspiring event, from which everyone leaves optimistic and full of confidence, assured that they have identified the goals, plans and tasks that will bring them the best results. And that is exactly the benefit for a salesperson creating a strategic plan. Salespeople spring up out of the strategic planning process confident that they have identified the most effective focus for their action, that they have identified the highest priority activities. They emerge confident, focused and optimistic, ready to take on the world (or at least their customers) with renewed vigor. And that's a good thing!

How to go about it.

1. Set aside, once a year, a significant amount of time dedicated to the task. I'd suggest at least a full day or two. The date of the strategic planning session should reflect the salesperson's selling situation. Salespeople vary in their seasonal "busyness" depending on the industry to which they sell. For some, a time towards the end of their fiscal year might be in order; for others, a time at the end of their busy season. For most, a time around the Christmas holidays works best.

One of my clients brings all his salespeople into the office for a planning retreat once a year. With another client, salespeople come together for an annual goal setting and strategy developing retreat. At this three-day event, they meet with their sales manager and create specific goals for the year. Then, together with the manager, they jointly develop the overall strategy for achieving those goals. If your company organizes such an event, good for you. If not, then you need to do it yourself.

2. Find a space where you can work virtually uninter-rupted. This may take some creativity. I doubt if it's your company office. It may be your home if you have a room in which you can isolate yourself.

    One year, I was one of two people responsible for leading an organization. The two of us drove to a state park, climbed in the back of my old conversion van, and worked in the back of the van all day long. We were isolated and uninterrupted.

3. Gather the materials you'll need: all your account folders, account profiles, your company's goals for the year, information about key products, services, or categories, computer print-outs of last year's sales, maps of your geographical territory, and anything else you may want to review.

4. Immerse yourself in the process. For the duration of the planning, don't do anything else other than emer-gency tasks. You want to focus your thinking on the strategic decisions you'll be making. Any interruption will disrupt your thinking.

5. Focus on what you are going to produce in this planning event – the output or result of your efforts. You are going to create these things:

    A. A set of sales goals for your territory.

    B. A well-defined ABC analysis of your customers and prospects.

    C. Individual goals and strategic plans for each of your key (A) accounts.

    D. A basic territory plan.

Sounds arduous, and it is. But, when you spend disciplined, focused time thinking about these things in detail, you will find it to be much easier than it looks. You will prepare the best, most effective plans of which you are capable, and that will free you to implement effectively when you are in the field.

Later in the year, you won't be tempted to head out on Monday morning without a clear plan in mind, because you have spent this time formulating the plan. And when the press of customer problems and inquiries threatens to overwhelm you and force you into becoming too reactive, you'll be held on track by the goals and plans you created in your planning discipline.

Outcomes

Let's consider each of these four outcomes of your planning retreat.

1. A set of sales goals for your territory.

Your work should lead you to a series of sales goals for your territory. In order to get there, you must first determine the categories of goals that you are going to create. It may be that you work for a company that has already determined this, like my clients described above. If so, good for you. If not, then it will be up to you to determine your own set of categories. Depending on your unique set of products and services as well as your company's emphasis, you may create goals for the following, most frequently used, categories:

A. Total sales

B. Total gross margin

C. Number of units

D. Total sales per product category (dollars, gross margin, or units) for each of several categories of product or service that you sell.

E. Goals for acquiring new accounts.

This is just a list of the most common sales goals. You can have a virtually unlimited variety of goals. The categories of goals are up to you, your company, and your manager.

I'd suggest no more than five categories. Remember, one of the reasons you create goals is to help you focus your energies on the most important issues, and thus become more effective. More than five goals defeat that purpose. Too many goals cause you to diffuse your energies, not focus them.

Let's illustrate. Assume that I sell sophisticated cleaning equipment and supplies to three different market segments: manufacturers, school systems, and shopping malls. My product line consists of a series of heavy-duty floor cleaning machines and the associated supplies used by those machines. I select the following categories to create goals:

1. Total sales

2. Total number of cleaning machines

3. Total number of "Superscrubbers," our new, high-tech machine

4. Number of new accounts

5. Total sales of supplies (as opposed to equipment)

Now that you have determined which categories on which to focus, you need to create specific numbers for each. This is where the "art" comes in. You consider your company's goals, you consider your understanding of what the market is doing, you factor in your best understanding of what your competitors are doing, and you consider your customers' situations and yours. Out of this comes your best attempt to predict a result that will cause you to stretch, but not be unreasonable.

I prefer to look at each account individually, think about it, and determine its likely contribution to each of the categories. Examine each account, analyze the potential, consider your situation, and determine a realistic goal. Go on to the next account, and do the same. Then compile each of the numbers from the specific accounts, and presto! You have an annual number.

Back to the example. Let's say we've done this, and come up with a set of annual goals that looks like this:

1. Total sales = $1,765,000

2. Total number of cleaning machines = 71

3. Total number of "Superscrubbers" = 16

4. Number of new accounts = 10

5. Total sales of supplies = $1,000,000

Now you are ready to move onto the next step.

2. A well-defined ABC analysis of your customers and prospects.

When it comes to strategic planning for salespeople, one of the most important strategic exercises is determining in which accounts you want to invest the bulk of your sales time. Too many salespeople become very reactive in their decisions, responding to whoever happens to be on the other end of the phone. Others find themselves in a route-type rut, mindlessly traversing their sales territory out of habit.

The cure to both of these is to strategically think about the potential of each account, and then to rank each account into one of three categories based on its potential. I describe a system to do this in Chapter Six of my book, *10 Secrets of Time Management for Salespeople.*

The result of this exercise is to have graded each of your prospects and customers as either "A" (highest potential), "B" (medium potential), or "C" (lowest potential).

3. Individual goals and strategic plans for each of your key (A) accounts.

If you are in the kind of selling position where you are attempting to sell more to certain key accounts, then you need to create specific, monthly strategic plans for each of those key accounts. For now, let's assume that you have prioritized your accounts and that you have a list of your "A" accounts.

In the typical sales territory, around 50 – 80% of your business is going to come from this group of accounts. That means that these accounts warrant special attention, special preparation, and special thought. You ought to apply the disciplines we have already discussed to your "A" accounts. In other words, create annual sales goals for each "A" account, and think about how you are going to do that, one account at a time.

4. A basic plan for your territory.

You have, at this point, decided what you want to do (your goals), with whom you want to do it, (your ABC categories), and how you are going to do that (your key account plans).

Now, it's time to put all this thinking together into an implementation plan. This is your basic plan for the use of your sales time. Where are you going to be on Monday? How will you manage that trip to the outer reaches of your territory? When will you schedule office time?

Lay out your basic schedule of how you are going to travel your territory. Make sure that you focus your time and attention on the A accounts, and that you work in time for the achievement of all your goals.

When you have done that, you will have created a salesperson's strategic plan. This annual exercise in discipline and thoughtfulness will serve you well, guiding you to the most effective use of your time, and keeping you focused on those activities that will bring the greatest result. And that is well worth your time.

Q #7. Dave, I do a good job of creating annual goals for myself. However, I'm finding it difficult to do the same for my personal finances. As a commissioned salesperson, my income varies from month to month. It seems like I'm always struggling with finances. Do you have suggestions for me?

A. Congratulations for having the courage to ask that question. Do I have suggestions? Yep, a bunch of them.

First, a little perspective, so you know where I'm coming from. For almost my entire adult life, I have been a commissioned salesperson whose income varied from month to month. Even now, my income varies monthly. So, I can certainly understand your situation on the income side. On the expense side, there have been times when I had obligations that at times seemed overwhelming. My wife was a full time homemaker, we raised a family of five children, and for many of those years I also had child support payments. Those were heavy financial responsibilities.

In all of this, I have learned some things about managing personal finances. Here are some of the lessons I have learned along the way.

First, as much as possible, avoid debt. Debt adds tremendously to your stress. You know that you must make those payments or you are going to have lots of unpleasant consequences. That may be constantly on your mind, contributing to sleepless nights and rising blood pressure.

Debt reduces your options. If you have monthly payments, for example, they must be paid even if you have a bad month or two. Without those payments, you can generally find a way to ride out low income months by temporarily reducing your standard of living. You can eat in every day, for example, instead of buying pizza or going out. Without monthly payments, you can even survive a few months of no income at all.

And the interest you pay eventually reduces your standard of living, because your interest payments are expenses that bring you no value.

So, be careful about putting anything on that charge card. And if you do, try to pay it off each month. Deciding to make just minimum payments is one of the most expensive decisions you'll ever make.

Also, be careful about any long term commitments. Instead of a three year lease on a new car, think about buying used and paying it off in two. Instead of a two year lease on that apartment, try 12 months. You may not ever be able to be totally debt free. However, you can make decisions which, over time, will significantly reduce your amount of debt, easing the pressure on you and allowing you more options.

Second, develop a monthly budget for reasonable living. In good months, don't spend the excess; put anything you make above that amount into a savings account. In bad months or years, tap into that savings account to meet your budget. At the end of the year, use some of the excess that you've build up to make those big purchases that you were tempted to put on a charge card during the year.

For example, say that you set up a budget of $3,000 a month. In January, you take home $3,400. Of that, $400 goes into the savings account, and you live on $3,000. In February, you take home $3,500. You repeat the discipline, putting $500 away. In March, you take home $2500. You take $500 out of the savings for your day-to-day expenses. When you've built up a comfortable surplus, buy those big things that you'd like to have.

This is one of the best things that I ever did. Even to this day, my wife and I operate on a budget. Here's an example. We have a certain amount of money dedicated each month to "entertainment." We use this for meals out, concerts, etc. When the money's gone, we're done. If we want to go out to eat, but don't have any money in the entertainment budget, we don't go. It's called deferred gratification, and it's the secret of surviving financially in a turbulent environment.

A number of years ago, I was involved with a group that had an excellent budgeting system, and taught it in small groups that met in homes. If you are interested, check out Crown Ministries.

Finally, one last thought. This will sound counter intuitive, but I have followed this rule for all of my adult life, and have found it to be extremely powerful. That rule is this: In times of economic uncertainty, increase your giving.

There is something about giving that helps you put your situation into perspective. It focuses you on people around you who need help in ways that you don't. It gives your family a broader perspective, injects new purpose into your life, and encourages everyone to be less self-centered.

Realize that I'm coming at this from a Christian perspective. There is a promise in the Bible that says we cannot out give God. When we give of our time and talents, God will respond by returning to us much more than what we have given. I have found that promise to be as bankable as my paycheck.

You may not share my perspective. Regardless, just from a purely pragmatic point of view, there are still some very practical reasons to increase your giving. When you get involved in some volunteer organization, you mix with a different group of people than that with which you are accustomed. New people, new situations, new issues are all invigorating for salespeople. Also, you'll find through your investigation of places to donate time and money to, lots of people who need help a whole lot more than you do. That helps you put your situation into perspective. And that helps you stay positive, optimistic and effective.

Think of giving in two ways: giving of your money, and donating your time and talent.

If you have some organization, cause, church or synagogue to which you regularly donate, consider increasing your donation. If you don't, now is the time to find some place to donate some of your money.

Find something in which you can donate your time. If you are not involved in some volunteer work, change that. Find someplace to give of your time and talents. For a number of years my wife and I were foster parents, caring for a total of 19 children of various ages, races, and emotional and physical disabilities. It kept us humble, broadened our lives, and taught us a lot. I'd recommend you find something like that – something into which you can invest your time and talent.

It really is the difficult times in your life, and your reaction to them, that shape your character and make you a better person.A *strategic plan* is composed of a set of measurable goals, coupled with a list of the most important, most effective things you (or your company) can do to reach those goals.

5

RELATIONSHIP BUILDING

Relationship Building: Eight Powerful Rules
(Excerpted from How to Excel at Distributor Sales Copyright 1995, 2000 by Dave Kahle)

Distributor salespeople must be better at relationship building than salespeople in any other type of selling situation.

You see your customers more often, and for longer periods of time than almost any other type of salesperson.

This means that you must build relationships that provide you a competitive edge over all of your competition.

Imagine this. You walk into a standing appointment with one of your largest customers. The receptionist greets you by your first name, and asks about your family. The main decision maker calls you right in, while one of your competitors sits in the waiting room. You visit together for about an hour, during which time he shares some information about new items coming up on the budget, and suggests you see one of the department managers who is having a problem.

You discuss a new product line your company recently acquired, and he indicates that the prospects are good for them to use it. He suggests price levels which would make your new product line attractive to the account.

57

While you're in his office, he calls and makes two appointments for you — one with the department head, and the other with the main decision maker for the new product line.

> *The result of your skillful relationship building is that you have earned your customer's comfortable preference. That's your competitive edge.*

You decide to go to lunch together. As you walk out, you see the competitor salesperson is gone. Over lunch, you don't mention business, but just talk about personal things. You genuinely enjoy each other's company.

That's what the fruits of powerful relationship building look like.

The result of your skillful relationship building is that you have earned your customer's *comfortable preference.* That's your competitive edge. With everything else being equal, you get the business. In a world where the distinctions between your company and your competitors are growing less and less clear to your customer, your relationship may be your only real competitive edge.

Often, the only reason a piece of business goes to one salesperson or the other is the depth and length of the personal relationship. They like you. So you get the business. Relationship building, then, is a key competency for success in the 21st Century.

In order to achieve mastery of this competency, you must follow an overriding strategy — to make yourself important to your customers. What does it mean to be important to your customers? It means being seen by the customer as a difficult to replace, integral part of his business and his job. Doing so gives you value to your manufacturers as well as to your customers.

When it comes down to the most basic values, do you know what a manufacturer really wants from you?

It doesn't matter how efficient your distribution systems are, nor how powerful your computers. Those are nice, but from the manufacturer's perspective, they're icing on the cake. What they really want from you is access to the customer. If you are important to your customers, you have more access to them than your competitor. And that's called job security.

The more important you are to them, the more important you are to your manufacturers. You operate as a middleman in an extremely powerful and effective way.

In order to <u>earn</u> this importance, you will have to implement the following eight rules for relationship building.

Eight Rules for Relationship Building

1. Give first.

Remember the law of reciprocity? It may be one of the single most powerful laws that govern human behavior for salespeople. The law simply states that people will act towards you the way you first act toward them. If you want good information and honesty from them, you must first provide good information and honesty to them.

In every meeting with a customer, try to bring something of value. It can be an idea, like what someone else is doing with a product or service you offer. It can be a story about a new product, or a new program. It can be something you read in an industry journal, or a clipping from a trade journal that has an idea your customer can use. The important thing is to try, at every meeting, to bring something of value.

As you consistently do this, a couple of things will happen. First, your customers begin to see you as someone other than "just a salesperson." Rather, they see you as a valuable associate, someone who really understands their business and has their best interests in mind.

Next, they begin to look forward to your visits, knowing that you'll bring something of value with you. After a while, they'll take your calls graciously, and try to make time to see you.

Additionally, when you give first, it creates a subconscious debt on their part. After a while, they feel like they have to return the gift with a piece of business or competitive information from which you can benefit.

This rule has a corollary. If you're always committed to giving first, it implies that if you don't have something of value to bring, you won't attempt to see your customer. Never take up their valuable time unless you have a legitimate, valuable item (valuable from their perspective, not from yours) to discuss.

Respect for your customers' time gradually creates a respect for yours in them. After a while, they'll see you every time you ask because they know that you have something of value to discuss. Your reputation precedes you — and that's a reputation you have consciously built with discipline and forethought.

2. Avoid failure.

Simple enough. But like most of the simplest, most basic rules, we often violate it.

My father was a salesperson. Interestingly, he was a salesperson for a distributor. I remember, as a child, spending the day with him. I was 8 or 10 years old, and it was my first taste of distributor sales. I clearly remember talking to him after one of his sales calls. He said, "Your enemies don't buy from you."

What a simple observation. But what profound implications. Of course! Your enemies don't buy from you. So, whatever you do, avoid making enemies. Do just the opposite — make friends instead.

Making enemies is failure. Don't get thrown out. Don't aggravate people to the point where you make them an enemy. Don't be so strong and so pushy that you make an enemy. Enemies won't buy from you. Avoid failure.

I learned about avoiding failure by failing. At one point in my career, I sold surgical staplers. At the time, this was a new concept for surgeons, and it had to be sold in a novel way. Our first task was to sell ourselves into the hospital operating room suite, and then we sold ourselves into the surgeons' lounge. There, we changed out of our street clothes and into greens. We hung around the surgeons' lounge, drinking coffee and waiting for the right surgeons to come in. When one would come in to change clothes to get ready for surgery, we would approach him and demonstrate the staplers. Then we'd say "Now doctor, if you would like to try this, I'd be happy to scrub your next case with you."

And we did. We took part on the surgical team, standing right next to the surgeon — gowned and gloved and "scrubbed" like the others. At that point, we had an opportunity to sell our equipment.

My lesson came when I was a little too strong in one hospital. The Chief of Surgery said to the OR supervisor, "Get him out of here." I left and was not welcome back there because I made an enemy. I failed.

I learned that I must keep the door open no matter what. The long-term relationship is always more important than the short-term sale. No single deal is worth jeopardizing the relationship.

3. Add to trust.

See people only when you have something worthwhile to see them about.

We distribution salespeople often get caught up in the activity and the regularity of our sales calls. In other words, we spend much of our time going through the motions, out of habit. For example, we may see a certain customer every Tuesday at 10:00 A.M. We mindlessly go through the motions.

To overcome this tendency, *have a reason* to see each person each time. Make sure you have something worthwhile to talk to them about. If you don't, then don't see them. Bring something worthwhile every time so you build up trust. They know you will not waste their time. And, time is the commodity of the '90s. It's the most important thing your customer has. Respect their time, and they'll respect you.

4. Reduce the risk of every decision.

The biggest issue in the minds of your customers and prospects is risk. Whenever you present them with a decision to make, the biggest thing they're thinking about subconsciously is risk. It's not just the money; it's the social, psychological and emotional cost that is also at risk.

In order to see this issue from your customers' perspective, you need to calculate the amount of risk that you expect your customers to take when you offer them an opportunity to say "yes" to you. You can then work to reduce that risk. The lower the risk of the decision, the more likely your customer will say "yes."

Here's an illustration to help you understand this concept. Imagine that you are under orders by your spouse to pick up a package of disposable cups on the way home from work today because you're having friends over for dessert and drinks tonight. You stop at the local grocery store, and make a selection between brand A and brand B. You pick brand A.

When you bring them home, your spouse mixes up a pitcher of margaritas and pours one. The drink leaks out of the bottom of the cup and puddles on the counter. There is a hole in the bottom of the cup. You pour your drink into another cup and it leaks, too. In fact, every one of the cups you bought is defective.

What happens to you in this instant in time? What is the consequence of your decision? I don't know about you, but I would be the recipient of some negative emotion. That may be the most painful cost of your decision. But there are other costs.

You're going to have to fix the problem. If there's time, you'll have to run back to the store and replace the cups. So, in addition to the emotional cost, you must pay in terms of extra time and additional money. All because of your bad decision. You accepted that risk when you made your decision.

Here's a simple exercise to help you understand this concept. Draw a short vertical line. At the top of the line write the number 25. At the bottom, write the number zero. Now on a scale of 0 - 25, where would you put the risk of buying a package of disposable cups? It's close to zero.

At the other end of the scale, I have an adoption agency as a client. When a young lady is in a crisis pregnancy, and she's making a decision whether or not to release her unborn child for adoption, how big a risk is that for her?

Most people say that it's a 25. It's a lifetime of consequences for at least four people. That's a very high risk. The point of this exercise is that when you ask your prospects to say yes to you, they are accepting some risk. Each decision you ask of them carries with it a different degree of risk.

Imagine a typical prospect. Then think of the typical offer or decision you ask of that person. Now, put yourself in his shoes, and see the situation through his eyes. On the 0 - 25 scale, how much risk does he accept when he says "yes" to you?

Here's an easy way of calculating it. Just ask yourself what happens to that individual if you, or your company, messes up.

If the risk to that person is high, then you need to work to reduce that risk.

If you want to build relationships in the 21st Century, look at every time you offer something to your customer and ask, "How do I reduce the risk?"

The winners in the competitive game are people who provide the same product or service at less risk. Reducing risk is a strategy for building relationships. If your prospect sees you as the lowest-risk source, he becomes comfortable with you. The relationship develops on the basis of this issue of risk.

5. Be remembered favorably.

Try to end every interaction you have with a customer on a positive note. And that generally means with some kind of an agreement. When you get into this mindset, it's not difficult to do. For example, a customer may call with a backorder problem. You say you'll check it out and call back tomorrow. You ask, "Will that be okay?"

When he says "Okay," you have reached an agreement and you have ended the interaction favorably. This constant positive ending is an important factor in building positive relationships.

Here's an example from my personal experience. I recently changed car insurance after 15 years with the same company. I made the decision on the basis of price. Although I was delighted with the service my previous supplier had provided, the difference in price finally became more than I could justify.

So I switched my business. Then I called my former agent and told her. In that conversation, she said she appreciated the reason I was switching and could certainly understand. She appreciated me as a customer and asked if there is ever anything she could do for me to please call. She then said if there was any way she could facilitate the transfer, please tell her how she could help. Finally, she said that if I ever had a question about insurance to feel free to call her.

You can imagine how I felt. I wish she would have reacted angrily; that way I wouldn't have felt so bad. But, instead, she ended the interaction favorably. Now I look for my new company to mess up so I can give her back the business. That's a great example of ending every exchange favorably.

6. Keep the relationship process moving forward.

Remember the chart showing the progression from "Suspect" to "Partner?" Not only does that model provide a neat way to think about your job, but it can also be a working set of objectives that govern every meeting you conduct with customers and prospects.

Your job, and your objective for every meeting, is to move people ever closer in a relationship with you.

Once you set your mind on the objective of continually moving people closer and closer to you, you'll find countless ways to do it.

> *Your job, and your objective for every meeting, is to move people ever closer in a relationship with you.*

However, if you never crystallize that as an objective, your relationship building will be happenstance rather than directed.

7. Broaden the relationship to include your company.

A good relationship with a customer is larger than just you. It's a relationship between companies as well as between people. It's important to have a personal relationship, that's part of the strength of what a distributor does, but realize that the companies have to have a relationship, too.

Facilitate that broader relationship at every occasion. Whenever you can arrange it, bring your managers in to see your customers. And do the opposite also. Bring your customers to see your facilities. The broader the relationship, the stronger it is. The more your customers know you, the more comfortable they are with you, and the more likely they are to do business with you.

8. Operate with 100% integrity.

In my first professional sales position, I learned a powerful lesson: complete honesty is not only morally right, it is good business.

People deal with people they trust. Complete honesty gives people reason to trust you. Lie to a customer, and they'll likely never forget it.

But integrity means more than just honesty. Integrity for a salesperson means that you do what you say you're going to do. You don't make promises quickly, you never promise something you're not sure of, you never over- promise, and you continually under-promise.

If you under-promise, you're in the position of always being able to deliver more than what your customer expected. That's an extremely powerful long-term relationship building strategy.

Integrity means that you never knowingly recommend something to a customer that you know isn't right for him. Remember, the long-term relationship is always more important than the short-term gain from an individual deal.

Finally, integrity means that you never speak badly about anyone, including your cheesiest competitor. It's a funny thing about judging someone — it always tells the person to whom you're speaking more about *you* than it does about the person who is the subject of your scrutiny. Talk badly about someone, and the person you're talking to wonders if you'll say the same thing about him when you're talking to someone else.

If you're going to build solid relationships with your customers, be someone who is worth their trust and their time. Integrity gives you that standing.

Q #8. *Since spending time face-to-face with customers is the best use of my sales time, how much of my week should I spend entertaining customers, taking them to lunch, ballgames, etc.?*

A. Great question. Let me answer this in two ways. First, spend as much time as you can interacting with your customers in social settings. That means that you should try to have lunch with a customer every day. You should entertain in the evening as often as your family, your boss, your lifestyle and your budget will allow.

Having said that, here's a second answer. The issue has more to do with the quality of the time than it does the quantity of time. You shouldn't spend social time with a customer just to meet some quantity goal. It's not time for the sake of time; it's time for the sake of some objective. If, for example, you take the same customer out to lunch every week because the two of you are buddies, that's not quality time. If you take people out to lunch or to a ball game, and those people are minor players in an account, having little, if any, influence on the decision, that also is not quality time.

Instead, I'd like you to be thoughtful and strategic about your investment of time in your customers. Make a list of all the people who are important decision-makers or influencers in your "A" accounts. Then, think about which of them do not know you very well. This is a critical issue. Remember, it's less important that you know them, than it is that they know you. If they feel like they know you and are comfortable with you, you will have significantly advanced the personal relationship and made it easier for them to do business with you. So your primary objective in spending social time with a customer is to have them become comfortable with you. Your secondary objective is to get to know them better.

With that clearly in mind, identify those powerful people in your "A" accounts who should know you better, and try to spend social time with them.

If I found myself free for lunch on Tuesday, for example, I'd start at the top of the list, and invite my number one candidate. If he/she couldn't make it, I'd go to number two, and so on. That way, I was always focusing on those individuals who were most strategically important.

The amount of entertaining by salespeople has dwindled significantly in the last decade. I recall one of my friends, a manufacturer's rep who sold automotive components in Detroit, had an entertaining budget in excess of $80,000 annually. And that was in the 1980s.

While those days of lavish spending are in the past, it is nevertheless true that spending social time with a customer can be a powerful sales strategy. In my days as a field salesperson, I would take two or three customers and their spouses out to dinner at Greektown in Detroit, followed by a Tiger game. My spouse would join me, and we would have six or eight people together for the evening. We never talked business, but business in those accounts always grew afterward. It was because they got to know me on a personal basis. I met their spouses, and they mine. We came to know one another as real people, not just people playing the role of buyer and seller. As a result of forging this personal relationship, it was easier for us to do business together.

That is still true today, perhaps even more so. As more and more business is done electronically, people hunger for the high-touch of personal relationships that have been excluded by high-tech communications. That salesperson who is able to build real personal relationships with his/her customers will succeed where others fail.

Q #9. How do you go over a person's head without making them angry?

A. I'm careful about ever going over someone's head in regards to some specific issue. You may win a battle but lose the war. Also, more times than not, the supervisor will support his/her subordinate's position. So, often, when you go over someone's head, you wind up making two enemies, not just one. Having said that, it is a solid strategy to create relationships with people as high up in the organization as possible.

If you have a pre-existing relationship with the head person, you can then access that person's position on any one issue and do it in a way that seems more like normal business than related to any specific issue.

One other thought. Your question implies that you are in the right, and your contact is wrong, and if you could only get to his/her boss, that person would see the light and buy from you. This is a very common misconception on the part of salespeople. Since you only see the situation from your perspective, you may not be aware of a number of issues that are important to the customer and that may impact the buying decision.

I'd suggest you go into that account with the mindset that there are reasons here that are holding up the purchase that you do not know about. Find out what else is on the customer's mind, and see if you can address those issues.

Q #10. If the time allowed for a sales call is too short, should you cancel or reschedule?

A. Good question. To put my answer in perspective, remember that I believe that time is the customer's scarcest asset. They never have enough time. That's why they use voice mail, and gate keepers - to help them get the most out of their days. It is so difficult to actually get face-to-face selling time that I believe any time should be treasured.

I've said all of that in order to say this: Take the appointment, even if you know you don't have enough time to do what you want to do. That gives you an opportunity to make a personal contact, and to help the customer get to know you and your product better. Do as much as you can during that first appointment, and, before you leave, make an appointment for the next visit to complete what you started.

Q #11. *You've said on several occasions that the most important part of my job is interacting with the customers. How important is it to spend time with the customers out of the office, and what percentage of time should I spend doing it?*

A. So many of these answers begin with the phrase "it depends." This is another one of them. The amount of time and money you spend entertaining customers, or spending time with them outside of the office, depends on the value of the account. The larger the annual dollar potential, the more time you should seek to spend with the customer on a personal level.

For example, if you sell water softeners to homeowners at $1,000 each, you probably should not ever invest in entertaining. On the other hand, if you sell those same water softeners to retailers, and one particular retailer could buy 2,000 of them in the course of the year, you should seek to deepen the relationship with that customer.

So, the answer begins with you analyzing the dollar potential of each of your accounts, and then making the determination as to which accounts, if any, are worth your extra investment of time and money. After you've compiled a "hit list" of people with whom you'd like to spend some additional time, create an annual budget. This can vary from a couple hundred dollars for lunches over the course of a year, to something entirely different than that. I recall a friend of mine who was a manufacturer's rep in the automotive industry, with General Motors as his only account. In the by-gone-days of lavish entertainment, he had an annual entertainment budget of $80,000.

After you have compiled your "hit list" and developed a budget, you then need to determine what that customer could do. Some accounts have policies against having lunch with vendors, for example. Others don't. Don't create an awkward situation by inviting your customer to do something that the company's policy discourages.

Ideally, I'd like to see you have breakfast or lunch every day with a customer. That's a good use of time for both of you. Try to schedule events – concerts or sporting events are always good, and invite your hit list. Be careful about outright gifts. You don't want to be seen as "bribing" anyone. Instead, orchestrate time together so that you nurture and expand the relationship.

Hope this helps.

Q #12. Dave, I have read your comments about the value of entertaining, and I agree with you. But, I have a problem. I still find a percentage of customers who keep me at "arms length." How do I overcome this attitude from the select few of my customers?

A. I have ideas to share with you on a couple of levels.

First, it is possible that you may never create good relationships with a certain percentage of your customers. I'm assuming, of course, that you are not an abrasive, insensitive clod. If you are sincere, professional and committed to developing excellent business relationships, and if you have a modicum of people skills, then you can reasonably expect to successfully build excellent business relationships with most people. There are almost always, however, some customers who won't respond to you because of issues on their side of the equation.

One of my former customers, for example, kept me at "arms length" for the five years that I called on him. Later, I learned that my competitor was his brother-in-law. No matter what I did, I could not compete with the depth of the social relationship with that competitor. They had Sunday dinners together regularly, and often vacationed together. The obstacles to developing the relationship were not in me; they were all on his side.

So, the first thought is this: Sometimes there is nothing you can do about it, because the issues are on their side of the relationship.

I believe that one of the principles of sales is that you don't sell them all. That's what makes the profession of sales so challenging. In the same sense, you don't create relationships with all of them. I think the mature salesperson recognizes that there are times and circumstances in which there are more fertile fields to plow, and then makes a strategic business move to focus on more responsive customers.

Having said that, however, it may be that, for whatever reason, you've decided to give it your best effort – that the potential is worth the extra time and effort that it will require.

If that's the case, then here are two suggestions for you. First, keep trying, but think outside your usual ideas and try something different. Here's an example. One of my customers was a middle-aged lady who just didn't like me. She was the primary influencer in a very large account, and my lack of a positive business relationship with her kept me on the outside of that account. For two years she rejected my invitations to have lunch or breakfast. It was time for something different.

My company owned six season tickets to the University of Michigan football games, and it was my turn to use them. I invited her and her spouse and one other customer and his spouse to attend with my wife and me. I am sure, in retrospect, that the only reason she accepted the invitation was that this was probably the only time in his life that her husband would have an opportunity to attend a U of M football game.

The six of us spent close to eight hours together, including the tailgate dinner before, the travel time and the game itself. I'll spare you the details. The day proved to be the turning point in the relationship, as we got to know one another in a social setting. From then on, the relationship improved and that account became one of my best accounts.

Doing something different – a football game with spouses invited — turned out to be the key to turning the tide.

That's suggestion one. Here's two: Focus on building a positive relationship with someone else inside the organization, and then leveraging that to influence the difficult customer.

Another example. One of my accounts was presided over by a crusty, irritable guy who had no use for me. He was the materials manager and the most important person when it came to dispensing purchasing contracts. I could get nowhere with him.

So I focused on building relationships with a couple of the younger people who reported to him. That went well. It was easy and natural for the three of us to go out to lunch together, and on several occasions, to invite him along. He came, and I was able to use that time to break down some of the walls.

Later, after I had taken the younger people to a baseball game, I invited him and his spouse to attend a game with my wife and I and another customer couple. The evening went very well, and he and his wife even went out with us for a night cap after the game was over. As we were heading for our cars afterward, his wife approached me, with tears in her eyes, and thanked me for the evening, saying that "No one had ever done that for him before."

The lesson in that story was to build relationships with other people inside the account, and then to leverage those to include and influence your problem customer.

Hope that helps.

6

SELLING COMMODITIES

*"How do you create a perceived value to
differentiate yourself from the competition when
you are both selling a commodity?"*

That's a question I'm often asked in my seminars. It uncovers
a problem that is spreading to almost every industry. The rapid
pace of technological development and our ultra-competitive
global economy means that no one can keep a competitive edge
in their product for very long. Develop a hot new product or
service, and before you can take your first check to the bank, a
competitor has a hotter or cheaper version. As a result,
customers are more and more inclined to view your product or
service as a commodity – no real difference between you and
the next guy.

This complicates life for the salesperson. In some cases,
you are selling exactly the same thing as your competitor. I
spent a number of years selling for a distributor who sold, for the
most part, exactly the same products as four or five competitors.
Many of my clients work in this arena. Lumber distributors (a
piece of lumber is a piece of lumber), industrial fasteners (a
screw is a screw is a screw), petroleum (87 octane gasoline is
87 octane gasoline), etc. The list goes on and on.

In other cases, your product may not be exactly the same, but the customer views your product as a commodity with no real differences between what you sell and what your competitor offers. How much real difference is there between Coke and Pepsi after all?

Regardless of the situation in which you find yourself, the problem for the salesperson is the same – getting the business in the face of the customer's perception of your "me too" product or service.

> *Granted, your product may be exactly the same as the competition, but the totality of your offering may be dramatically different.*

So, what do you do? This. To put it simply, you must detail and communicate the important ways your offering differs from your competitors.

That's easier said than done. To do so effectively, you need to spend some time thinking and preparing. And that means that you must carefully consider the two most important elements of the sale – your offering, and your customer. In this article, I am going to focus on one part of that equation – your offering.

Granted, your product may be exactly the same as the competition, but the totality of your offering may be dramatically different. I use the word "offering" to indicate every aspect of the purchasing decision – not just the product. For example, the customer buys the product from a company – yours or the other guy's. The customer buys it from a salesperson – you or the competitor. Your company and you are part of the "offering." In addition, there may be differences in your terms, delivery, your customer-service capabilities, your follow-up, your return policy, your value-added services, etc. All of these are part of your "offering."

The product may be identical, but everything else about your offering may be different. For example, let's say you are contemplating purchasing a new Taurus.

You have identical price quotes from two dealers. The product is the same, and the price is the same. However, one dealer is close by, the other across town. One dealer has a reputation for great customer service; the other has no such reputation. The salesperson for the first dealer is the brother of an old high-school friend, while the salesperson for the second dealer is a bit cocky and pushy. The first dealer has a clean, comfortable establishment, while the second one is cramped, cluttered and dirty.

From whom do you buy your Taurus? Stupid question. Of course you buy it from the first dealer. Not because of any differences in the product or the price, but because of differences in the offering. Got the idea? There is a whole lot more to a decision to buy than just the product or the price.

Your first job is to identify those differences. Here are some very specific steps you can take today.

1. Think about everything that is associated with the product when a customer purchases it. Create several categories, and label columns on a piece of paper with the names of those categories. For example, the first column could be headed with the word "company," the second with the word "salesperson," the third with "terms." Continue in this way, identifying every aspect of the offering and placing each of those components at the top of a column.

2. Now, consider each column one at a time, and list all the ways that your offering differs from your competitor's in that column. For example, your company may be locally owned as opposed to your competitor's branch of a national company. Or you may be physically closer to the customer, or larger, smaller, newer, older, etc. After you've exhausted one column, move onto the others, filling in the details as you go.

3. This exercise will typically reveal dozens (and in some cases hundreds) of specific, detailed differences. Far too many than you can easily communicate to the customer. So, your next step is to pick out those differences that are most important to your customer. Keep in mind that often what you see as important may not be viewed that way by your customers.

At one point in my career, I worked for a company that celebrated its 100th year anniversary. That was unusual. No other competitors had been in business nearly that long. The company decided to make a big deal about it. A history of the company was written, brochures printed, even murals depicting significant moments in the company's history were painted on the walls of the corporate office. We all thought it was important.

Our customers, however, didn't care. After respectfully listening to our boasting, their response was some form of "So what?" In other words, our 100 years didn't mean anything to them. In no way did it make their jobs easier, simplify their lives, or make them more important to their companies. What we thought was important turned out to be irrelevant from our customers' perspective.

Don't make the mistake we made. Instead, take the time to critically analyze your list, and eliminate those items that are not important to your customer, that don't impact their jobs or make a difference to them. You should be left with a handful of items.

4.   One more step to the preparation. Translate each of those items into statements of benefit to the customer. For example, your company may be local, while your competitor ships from 50 miles away. So what? What does that mean to your customer? You could translate that item of difference into a benefit by saying something like this: *"As opposed to some other suppliers, we're just 15 minutes from your plant. This means that you can get quick delivery of emergency shipments, as well as rapid response to any problem that might develop. So, you'll have potentially less downtime in the plant, and of course, less stress and pressure on you."*

Now that you've professionally prepared, you are ready to communicate those differences to your customer. You need to point them out in an organized and persuasive presentation.

Prepare a sell sheet with each of the differences noted as a bullet. Next to each bullet, have a few comments that capsulize the benefit statements you prepared. Then, meet with your customer, lay the sheet down in front of him/her, and talk down through it, explaining each point as you go.

Treat it like you would any other well-done presentation. Be sensitive to your customer's reaction, and ask for feedback as you work down through the list. Say, "How does that sound?" or

"Does that make sense to you?" and emphasize those things that seem to be more important to your customer. Then, leave that sheet with your customer.

> *As always, if you have done a good job of analyzing, preparing, and communicating, your customer's perception should be altered, and you gain the business. If you haven't done well at this, then your customer will continue to see no difference between buying it from you and buying from the next guy.*

I'm always amazed at the number of salespeople who are confounded over the customer's perception that their product is just like the other guys, when those salespeople have done nothing to show the customer how it is different.

As always, if you have done a good job of analyzing, preparing, and communicating, your customer's perception should be altered, and you gain the business. If you haven't done well at this, then your customer will continue to see no difference between buying it from you and buying it from the next guy. And, if you haven't shown him/her sufficient reason to buy it from you, then he shouldn't.

From the customer's point of view, if your offering is just like the competitor's, then the customer is absolutely correct in buying from the cheaper source. However, if there is any difference between your offering and your competitors', then the responsibility is totally yours to show the customer that difference. Follow the process described here, and you'll have far fewer customers treating you like a commodity.

Q #13. How do you overcome the sales cost factor, when your competitor has a fax for a salesperson?

A. By this, I'm assuming that you mean that your competitor makes use of a fax to make a sales offer, while you are a live salesperson and your costs are higher than the fax machine. As a result, the competitors' prices are lower than yours are.

So, the question is, "Why should the customer pay more to buy the product from you?"

Look at it from the customer's point of view. If he/she perceives everything as being equal, he should buy it from the lowest price vendor. If you are going to ask for more money, you have to give him something he values to justify that additional price.

And that means that you must truly be a "consultant salesperson." If all you are doing is shooting the customer a price, a website or fax can do that just as effectively and a whole lot less expensively than you.

The solution then, lies in your approach to your job, and the skills that you bring to bear on behalf of the customer. Create solid personal relationships; ask better questions in order to understand the customer's deeper needs; present creative solutions that distinguish you from everyone else. In so doing, you gain the customer's respect and bring value to him/her.

I don't mean to make this sound easy. Most salespeople, myself included, spend a lifetime honing these skills and this "consultative" approach to selling. Our monthly TGIF& K seminars, all our video and audio tape educational programs, and most of my live seminars are designed to help you with this. Good luck!

Chapter Six ~ Selling Commodities

Q #14. I'm tired of my customers always trying to get a lower price. Anything I can do?

A. When was the last time you bought a car, a house, or any other major purchase and said, "Thanks, I'd be happy to pay full list price?" That probably has never happened. Whenever a good chunk of your money was involved, you tried to get it at a lower price.

That's just human nature. No one wants to pay more for something when there is a possibility that it is available at a lower price.

That's true for your customers as well. They wouldn't be doing their job if they didn't ask for a lower price.

So, don't be surprised if they ask for a lower price. Be surprised if they don't!

That said, the real question is, "What can you do to insure that you get the business at a decent price?"

Three thoughts:

1. **Focus on Exceptional Execution of the Essentials.**

   If you do an exceptional job of the essential behaviors of a professional salesperson, you'll have increased the likelihood that the customer will pay your full price.

   Over and over again, I find myself bringing salespeople back to the essentials of the job. And I discover, time after time, that almost every sales problem can be fixed or prevented by doing the essentials well.

   What are the essentials?

A. Building rapport and creating relationships such that the customer trusts you, knows you and is comfortable with you.

B. Learning about the customer's situation, needs, interests and motivations in a deeper and more detailed way than your competitors.

C. Presenting your solution in a thoughtful, well prepared and persuasive way.

D. Acquiring agreement on the next step at every point in the process. Do these things well, better than your competitor and you'll gain more business and prevent some of the "lower price" requests.

It sounds so simple, and in a sense it is. The problem is that we are never as good at these things as we can be. Constant improvement in the essentials is a never-ending process that should engage us for the rest of our careers. So many salespeople look for solutions in some cute phrase to say, some magic word, or some clever strategy. The answer so often is in our own exceptional execution of the essentials.

2. Dollars to benefits

At the point in which a customer asks for a lower price, one effective tactic is to compare the money they are spending to the benefits of your product. Try to express the dollars in the lowest possible way, and to maximize the benefits.

For example, you may be selling a piece of production equipment for $100,000. This particular piece of equipment can spit out 100 units per minute. You say something like this: "Over the next five years, this will cost you less than a tenth of a cent per unit. So, you'll receive quality processing for fractions of a penny per unit."

Notice that you broke the $100,000 into the lowest possible way of expressing that amount – "less than a tenth of a cent per unit." Then you compared that to the benefit they receive – quality processing.

This technique can put pressure on the customer to back off his/her request for lower prices.

3. Have a back-up plan

There are times when you need to make some price concession in order to keep the customer happy. At those times, you should have a back-up plan ready.

At one time in my career, I sold amplification equipment for classrooms of hearing-impaired children. My product was 30% more expensive than the other two competitors with whom I competed.

When there was a situation where the customer absolutely would not pay our price, we had a back-up plan. We bid our older series of equipment at the price that we thought would get the business.

So, if a customer wouldn't pay our price, we were ready with an option for them – a way to allow them to pay less, but that still provided us with a decent profit.

Take the time to work this out before you confront the low-price customer.

Hope this helps.

Q #15. *In a situation where I have made contact with the decision maker, I have provided samples and prices but it needs to go to the prospects' quality control department. Assuming that I have not been able to pre-schedule an in-person appointment or specific call back date for results, I end up wasting a tremendous amount of time to get one of three answers:*

    a. No thanks.

    b. QC still not done.

    c. Yes, I'd like to place an order.

I repeatedly call back and leave voice mail requests for an answer with no response. Any ideas of how I can be more effective in this scenario? Many salespeople simply keep returning physically to the customer to try to get an answer, but I don't think this is any more effective than phone calls.

A. Let's look at the situation from the customer's point of view. He probably has more important things to do than test your product. Your project has become a low-on-the-to-do-list item. He'll get to it when he gets to it.

Why isn't it any big deal to him? Because you haven't made it one. In your proposal to him, you haven't hit any sufficiently sensitive and intense hot buttons to motivate him to push the project out of the mode of standard operating procedures.

Let's say you've shown him that you can save him 3% on one component of his product. Yawn. That's nice, but you aren't going to unleash any torrents of energy devoted to pushing your deal through. And, really, from his perspective, does it make any difference if he decides to buy it today, or he decides to buy it next month? Probably not. So, your deal continually gets pushed down the ever growing and changing list of things he has to do.

So, the problem is that your customer isn't motivated to push your project ahead of other things he has to do. And the reason he isn't motivated is because you haven't given him a reason to be motivated.

The place to address this issue is not *after* you have made the proposal, it is *before*. Do two things. First, in your information collecting, concentrate on finding the prospect's hot button. Find some things about which the prospect is already passionate. Then when you make your proposal, show how your product helps him reach those goals and helps him achieve the things about which he is already passionate.

The issue is motivation, and you don't interject motivation, you discover it. Discover what he's already motivated about, and link your product to it.

Second, give him some reason to act by a certain date. Maybe you have a special price promotion, or some service that he would value, etc. There should be something the customer gains by acting by some date. So your proposal should be X if he orders before some date, and Y if he orders after. That gives him a reason to push your project up the to-do list. Then, when you call and get voice mail and leave a message, you can remind him of what is at stake if he makes the decision by that date.

If you are able to put either or both of these pieces into play, you'll find that most of the frustration with projects that linger forever is eliminated by preventing it on the front end of the sales process.

Good luck.

Q #16. *How do I insure that I get the last look in a competitive bid situation?*

A. This is a question that I'm often asked. In a lot of industries, particularly those involved in construction, government purchases and large-volume manufacturing, most of the customers require an official bid. It's not unusual for these to be highly formal and structured.

Here's a typical scenario. The customer sends a bid to five suppliers, and each responds with a written document by a certain specified date. The customer reviews the bids, and awards the business.

The writer of the question wants the ability to go in after the bids have been submitted, to look at the competitive bids or at least the lowest bid prices, and to change his/her prices in order to be awarded the business.

It should be noted, first, that in some instances, the "last look" is illegal. In many cases, it's viewed as unethical. In other industries and situations, it's viewed as business-as-usual.

I have responses for this on several different levels.

1. Avoiding a bid situation to begin with.

2. Making a last look unnecessary.

3. Insuring that you get a last look.

Let's think about each one separately.

1. Avoiding a bid situation to begin with.

Okay, I know that bids are standard operating procedures in your business. But, I also know that a lot of business is "negotiated." In other words, the customer selects the vendor he/she wants to work with, and then negotiates the best deal with that customer.

I'd much rather that you get yourself into *a negotiating* rather than a *bid* situation. So, you'd avoid the bid scenario altogether.

And, while it is true that you'll never convince 100% of your customers to negotiate with you rather than send out bids, if you are, over the next few years, successful in moving 20 – 30% of your customers to negotiating status, you'll see a tremendous improvement in your sales.

How do you earn that position? Build powerful business relationships, be a reliable supplier, and offer a special relationship – "negotiating" – with all your good customers.

In other words, bring the subject up regularly, plant the seed in your customer's brain, tell stories about how you were able to work effectively with others – how they cut costs, paperwork and time out of the cycle by working with you.

If you are good, and persistent, you'll eventually convert a significant chunk of your customers.

2. Making a last look unnecessary.

The whole concept of a "last look" implies that the reason the customer would do business with you is that you are the lowest price of the group of bidders. While there is a time and place to be the low price, I'd like for you to question whether or not this is how you'd like the customer to think of you. If you have done a good job in the past for the supplier, if you have become the low-risk supplier, if you have understood the customer's situation at a deeper level than your competitors, if you have some aspect of your product, service or offer that sets you apart from the competitors, if you have communicated those things in a persuasive way, then the customer should be happy to do business with you even if you are not the absolute lowest price.

In other words, if you have done a good job of selling, then a couple percentage points in the price should have no impact on the deal.

So, rather than try to be the low price, I'd prefer that you do a deeper, better job of selling this account so that you don't have to be the lowest price. And that means that you have created powerful, trusting relationships with the key people, that you have understood the dynamics of their situation at a deeper and more detailed level than any of your competitors, and that you have fashioned a unique proposal that meets their deeper needs.

When you do that, you don't need to worry about the last look.

3. Insuring that you get a last look.

Okay, some of your customers negotiate the business with you, and the last look is, of course, not an issue with them. Some of them will buy from you because of the good job of selling you did, and the last look, with them, is not an issue.

But you will still probably be left with those who are going to bid and award the business primarily on the basis of price. It's that group for which you'd like to have the last look.

How do you do that? By achieving excellence in the basics: building powerful, positive business relationships with those key contacts, by understanding their needs in deeper and more detailed ways than any of your competitors, by doing everything you can to assure that your company is highly respected by the customer, and finally, by asking for the opportunity.

What you are really asking for is the preference of the customer. You are assuming that there is no difference between you and your competitor, and there is no reason for the customer to pay a little more to do business with you. Your only hope is that the customer will prefer to do business with you, providing you are the lowest price. You want the customer to prefer to do business with you, so that they call you for a last look and potential revision of your proposal.

Ask yourself why the customer would prefer you. Then set about becoming the supplier with which your customer would want to do business. And, continually ask for the opportunity to have a last look.

Q #17. Occasionally, customers may say they have seen or received a lower price for the same product in order to receive better pricing from us. How would you handle that type of call?

A. You mean this only happens occasionally? I'll bet thousands of my readers see it frequently.

Regardless, there are a number of things you can do.

First, assess the validity of the customer's comment. Your question says that your customers "may say". That implies that sometimes, at least, you think they are just saying it, and not meaning it. So, you have to determine the likelihood that they really have seen the same thing at a lower price. If you think they are just making it up, and they really don't have a lower-price option, then just diplomatically ignore it. Say something like this, "I really don't know what else is available, but I do know that this is a fair price. Should I send you one or two?"

You'll never know if they are bluffing until you call their bluff. It's worth losing one or two to help you understand the reality of their comment.

Second, if you think that they really do have another lower-price option, then you need to spend some time in preparation before you even make the call, so that you will have a strategy and set of techniques ready for this situation.

Assess your position in the account. Ask yourself these two questions: "Are you the preferred vendor?" "If all things were equal, would they prefer to do business with you?"

If the answer is "Yes," and you are the preferred vendor, then that is usually worth at least 3%, but rarely more than 10%. In other words, if your competitor can sell it for $100.00, and you are the preferred vendor, you can probably get $103.00, but probably not $111.00 for the same product.

So, you need to determine if you are the preferred vendor and, if so, how much that is worth to the customer. Create a deal which in effect lowers the price to what you think you can get. Have that deal, plus some language to offer it, ready for the situation.

For example you might say, "I understand that you may be able to purchase it for less. Let me suggest this, when you buy item Y, we can provide it for $103.00 plus $8.00 for item Y. That gives you a discount from our regular prices, plus a great buy on item Y. Do you want to go ahead with that?"

That, of course, assumes that all things are equal. The truth is that all things are rarely equal. There is probably some reason why the customer should buy it from you. That means some benefit that the customer gets from the transaction with you that is valuable to him/her and that is not going to come from the competitor.

Just ask yourself the question, "Why should they do business with me?" And don't answer it from your perspective, answer it from theirs.

If there is nothing that the customer gets that is valuable to him, then he should not buy it from you. Once you identify the benefits to the customer of doing business with you, you then need to prepare a statement or two that capsulizes the reason why someone should buy it from you.

There are thousands of reasons why they should buy from you beyond just the price or the product itself. There is the state of the relationship, for example. They like you. That's reason enough. Or, maybe your invoices are clearer, your terms more flexible, your delivery more reliable, etc. Or, it may be just more convenient.

Here's an example. Almost every morning that I'm in the office, I first stop at the coffee shop on the first floor of my building and get a cup of coffee to bring to the office with me. It's good coffee, but no better than I can get several other places. But it is more expensive. In some cases, it's twice as much as I would pay elsewhere. Why do I intentionally pay more? Because it's convenient, I don't have to go out of my way to buy it, and the people in the shop know me and greet me by name. To me, those are nice benefits, and worth an extra $.50 a day.

So, while the product is the same, and the price more expensive, there are some reasons why I'm willing to pay the extra price.

Put yourself in your customer's shoes, and determine why they should pay the extra price to buy it from you. Take those reasons, and turn them into a persuasive sentence or two. Memorize those two sentences. Then, the next time someone offers the comment, you'll be ready to persuasively show them why they should still buy it from you.

Good luck!

7

DEALING WITH VOICE MAIL

Victory Over Voice Mail
(Excerpted from Take Your Performance Up-a-Notch
Copyright 1999 by Dave Kahle)

**Challenge: Voice Mail is driving me crazy! It seems like
I can never get through to the people I want to talk to**

Welcome to the club. Not so many years ago, there was no
such thing as voice mail. Today, it is almost impossible to call a
customer on the phone and get directly to him.

The electronic gatekeeper, voice mail, stands in the way.
Voice mail has become the number one irritant for salespeople
in the Information Age.

And with good reason. If you can't communicate with your
customers, you can't get to see them. And if you can't get to see
them, you've been knocked out of the sales process. Unless
you learn to work through this electronic obstacle, the likelihood
of you making a sale is dramatically reduced.

> *Voice mail has become the number one irritant*
> *for salespeople in the Information Age.*

So, voice mail is one of those irritating issues that threaten the very heart of what you do. You must solve the voice mail dilemma or you won't be in business very long.

Let's begin by recognizing that voice mail is one of the most likely outcomes of your telephone call. So, don't be surprised when you call a customer and are routed to voice mail. Instead, be prepared. Imagine that you are given the ability to create a 30-second radio commercial and beam it directly to your customer. What would be in that commercial?

That's the attitude to take. So, before you make each telephone call, prepare a 30 second radio commercial (your voice mail message). Then you're prepared for the likely occurrence of being routed to a voice mail system.

Next, put as much skill into your voice mail message as possible in order to influence the customer to take action. Begin by focusing on the action that you want the customer to take. If you're cold calling for a first appointment, the action you want the customer to take is to get back to you, either in person or via email or fax. If you're following up on a proposal or a previous visit, you want a different action from the customer. Keep clearly in mind the action you want them to take, and bring all your skills of influencing, using the presentation process as best you can, to deliver a powerful presentation. Don't sell your product, sell a return call. Give them a reason to call you back.

The presentation, like all of them, should traverse through the steps of the basic presentation process. Identify some need/ interest you believe your customer has, identify something you can do to assist him, show him how that will benefit him, and ask for action. Use your language and tone of voice to convey competence and confidence and to make your customer comfortable with you. It's the influencing-presentation process capsulized in 30 seconds.

Consider the possibility of creating a series of communications of which your voice mail message is merely one piece.

Think about using alternate media to make a series of contacts with the customer, to precondition him/her to respond to your call. For example, you may send a letter, follow it with an email, follow that with a fax, and then make your phone call.

A few years ago, one of my clients, an advertising agency, developed an incredibly creative way to precondition the customer to accept the initial phone call. Here's how the program worked. They first qualified a list of 100 people they wanted to see. During the first week of the program, they sent each of the 100 people a small box, wrapped in plain brown paper, with a hand-printed address on it, and no return address. In the box was a sugar cube with a small printed message saying, "Keep it sweet." Nothing else. You can imagine the curious response of the people receiving that box.

The second week, another package came in the mail. It was wrapped and addressed in the same way, only this time, the box contained a lemon. The message read, "Don't let it go sour."

Week three came, and a third box arrived. Same wrapping, same appearance. This package contained some tinsel foil with the message, "Make it sparkle." Week four arrived, and the anticipated delivery of the fourth box. In it was the business card of the salesperson with a note, "I'll be calling you for an appointment." You may be interested in the result. One hundred percent of the recipients of that series of packages set appointments with the sales reps. The electronic barrier of voice mail was overcome by creatively pre-conditioning the customer to respond to the call for an appointment.

But there are frequent occasions when you encounter voice mail and you're well down the road of the sales process. It's not your first call; it's a subsequent visit with a customer you know.

Think ahead and avoid voice mail altogether. When you're with the customer, instead of agreeing to call him and make an appointment for the next meeting, make the appointment now, while you are with the customer. Explain that doing so, even if it is tentative and several months in the future, will save you both a phone call or two, and that means less time and less hassle for both of you. When you make the appointment, you've eliminated the need for a phone call and the frustration of voice mail.

Even if the situation or one of your schedules changes, you can then use voice mail to your advantage by calling with a schedule change, leaving that message, and getting your customer's acknowledgment on *your* voice mail.

Q #18. How do I get to see new prospects who won't return voice mail?

A.1 This continues to be one of the most-asked questions I receive. I wish I could provide you with a magic phrase or set of "secret" words that are guaranteed to get the prospect to return your call and grant you an audience. But it is just not that easy. Influencing new prospects to return your call and to invest their time in the speculative venture of seeing another salesperson is not a simple thing. And, clearly, it is growing more difficult.

There is no one strategy, no simple guaranteed set of tactics that will work magic for you. There are, however, some principals and strategies that will increase the likelihood of you getting an appointment with the elusive prospect. Starting with this issue, I'm going to spend several months dealing with this challenge.

There is a principle that we need to grasp if we're going to be more effective at this most difficult task. The principle is this: There is no short cut, no simple, easy magic answer.

That means that you are going to have to invest serious planning time and serious creative thought in improving your results. To make it easier, I'm going to break my answers into several parts.

Let's start with this essential first step. Prepare a powerful opening statement. You use this to introduce yourself to a prospect as well as to leave as part of your voice mail message.

This statement should be short and persuasive. It should communicate specifically what benefit your company can bring to the prospect. I like this organization:

1. who you are

2. what you do for companies like your prospect's

3. the specific benefit for the prospect to see you

4. how much time you'll need

Here's an example: *"Hello..............., this is Dave Kahle, President of the DaCo Corporation. We are a consulting and training company that focuses on helping B2B companies increase their sales and develop their people. We have some unique resources that can help your salespeople improve their performance. I'll need about 15 minutes to share some of the resources that are applicable to......... companies like yours."*

You then ask for the appointment, if you are talking to a live person, or to return the call if you're leaving a voice mail message.

Notice, in this example, that we introduced ourselves, focused on a benefit for companies like this one, made it specific to this company, and then indicated how much time that customer would need to invest – all in about 65 words.

Also, notice that the benefit is very specific, "help your salespeople improve their performance." The more specific the benefit, the more attractive it is. So many times I hear salespeople make vague and general promises like "save you money." Your prospects hear these vague promises so often that they mean nothing. Instead of a vague promise, mention some very specific benefit.

This is just the first, necessary step in achieving more appointments. There are a number of other strategies that build on this.

In the next part, I'll expand on this most difficult challenge with some additional ideas. For now, work on creating a persuasive opening statement.

A.2 In the previous section, I talked about creating a powerful, persuasive opening statement. In this portion, I'm going to expand on the concept of an effective "pre-call touch."

First, a little perspective. I wish I could provide you with a magic phrase or set of "secret" words that are guaranteed to get the prospect to return your call and grant you an audience. But it is just not that easy. Influencing new prospects to return your call and to invest their time in the speculative venture of seeing another salesperson is not a simple thing. And, clearly, it is growing more difficult.

There is no one strategy, no simple guaranteed set of tactics that will work magic for you. There are, however, some principals and strategies that will increase the likelihood of you getting an appointment with the elusive prospect.

There is a principle that we need to grasp if we're going to be more effective at this most difficult task. The principle is this: There is no short cut, no simple, easy magic answer. That means that you are going to have to invest serious planning time and serious creative thought in improving your results.

Here's one option which is used effectively by a number of my clients. I call it an "effective pre-call touch."

What's a pre-call touch? It's a delivery that you make to the person with whom you are trying to gain an appointment. That delivery conditions them to be more receptive to your call.

There are several different kinds of pre-call touches. The first and most effective is a personal introduction. If you know someone who can introduce you personally, face-to-face, to the person you want to talk to, that personal introduction is always the most effective way of meeting a new person. Once you have your list of prospects, look through the names and ask yourself, "Is there anyone I know who might know some of these people?" If so, ask them to introduce you. If they agree, then you will have arranged for a very effective pre-call touch.

Next down the ladder of effectiveness is an introductory phone call. This is where someone you know calls someone who is on the list and suggests to them that they talk to you when you call. They introduce you over the phone and say good things about you. That's another very effective pre-call touch.

Here's a third one, called a pre-heat letter. This is a letter from someone else, to the person who you want to see, introducing you. In other words, instead of you just calling the person out of the cold, you have someone write them a letter.

This isn't as hard as it seems. My insurance agent does this with me. Here's how he works his system.

He calls and invites me to lunch once or twice a year. Of course I know that he wants to get some referrals from me.

After I agree to have lunch with him, he sends me a form a few days before the lunch. The form asks very specific questions, all asking who I know who meets certain criteria. My job is to list some names on this form. Then we go to lunch. At lunch we make small talk and catch up on each other's lives. Then somewhere toward the end of the lunch, my insurance agent pulls out his big folder and he says, "Now who do you know who I might see?" He asks me to refer to the form and read off the list of names.

So, I give him two or three names. That, however, is not the end of it. He next asks me about each of those people. He inquires into what I know about them, how old they are, what education they have, do they own their own business, etc. He collects pieces of information about each of those people. Then he says, "You wouldn't mind introducing me to them, would you?"

I say, "No, I guess not."

He says, "How about if I write a letter from you to them mentioning me and suggesting that if I call them they should take the call? I will write a letter from you and I'll have my secretary bring it over. All you have to do is sign it. Would that be okay?"

I agree to do that. Sometime in the next couple of days, in comes the secretary with two or three letters from me to the people whose names I just gave him, introducing my insurance agent to them. I sign them and she folds them up, slides them into an envelope and off they go. That's a great example of a pre-call touch, a letter from someone else that introduces you and conditions that person to accept your call.

Here's another type of pre-call touch: A delivery, or a series of deliveries, that come from you that softens the prospect and makes them more likely to receive your call. You can create a series of letters, or other creative deliveries, and send one, two, three, four, five letters beforehand, each emphasizing some aspect of what it is you sell. And by the time your prospect has read those letters or received your deliveries they should be open to talking to you.

I just received a great example of this. A Fed Ex overnight delivery appeared one day, personally addressed to me. The box contained a bottle of Pepsi, a bag of microwave popcorn, and a personal letter to me. The letter asked me to view a web-based presentation. Sit back, eat popcorn and have the Pepsi while I watch the presentation.

Now, I chose not to watch it. But that was because it was not a sufficiently interesting subject. I did, however, think favorably about the company that sent it to me. And, if they would have followed up with a phone call, I probably would have taken it.

That was a very effective pre-call touch – a delivery to the prospect conditioning him/her to accept your call.

Here's another possibility - a fax or an email to your prospect first, giving the prospect some reason to take your call. Send a fax or email and then follow it up with a call.

Finally, another very effective pre-call touch is a handwritten – not typed, not computer generated, personal letter from you to the prospect explaining what you would like to see them about and asking for an appointment.

Notice that all of these examples have some characteristics in common – they are creative deliveries made to the prospect that conditions him/her to be receptive to your call.

Your challenge is to take that definition and, stimulated by the examples I've given you, develop a creative "pre-call touch" of your own. If you'd like to share your ideas with me, please feel free to send me an email describing what you came up with. I may share it with others.

Good luck.

A.3 In the first section, I talked about creating a powerful, persuasive opening statement. In the previous portion, I discussed the concept of an effective "pre-call touch." In this section, I'm going to discuss some effective tactics for making the call.

First, a reminder of the perspective from which we should view this problem. It's this – there is no simple, easy solution. I wish I could provide you with a magic phrase or set of "secret" words that are guaranteed to get the prospect to return your call and grant you an audience. But it is just not that easy. Influencing new prospects to return your call and to invest their time in the speculative venture of seeing another sales person is not a simple thing. And, clearly, it is growing more difficult.

There is a principle that we need to grasp if we're going to be more effective at this most difficult task. The principle is this: There is no short cut, no simple, easy magic answer. There are, however, some principals and strategies that will increase the likelihood of you getting an appointment with the elusive prospect. That means that you are going to have to invest serious planning time and serious creative thought in improving your results.

Okay. You've prepared an effective opening statement, and you've sent a creative pre-call touch. Now you are going to make the call, using the opening statement that you have prepared, and making reference to the pre-call touch that you delivered. What are some ways to make the actual phone call more effective?

1. Time it right. You may have greater success in getting to your prospect by calling at an odd time. Try a few minutes before 8 AM, ditto for lunch, and a few minutes after 5:00 PM.

These are all times when the normal switchboard may not be operating, yet the person you want may be at his/her desk.

2. Practice a conversational voice. Don't sound too smooth or rehearsed. That makes the person listening to your voice mail think that you are just another salesperson. I've always found it more effective to sound a bit "real." It is okay to stutter a bit, to hesitate, to use an occasional "ah." All these make you sound like a real person, not an automaton repeating a memorized pitch.

3. Always leave a message. Imagine that you could buy a 15 second radio commercial that you could beam directly to your prospect. Wouldn't that be a good thing to do? That's what voice mail allows you to do. So, every time you encounter voice mail, deliver your radio commercial.

4. Show that you understand them. In your voice mail message, leave the name of a company similar to theirs that you have dealt with, or mention a very specific problem that you believe they have, or some individual that you have worked with who they may know.

Another approach is to ask a penetrating question. That's a question that indicates your knowledge of the prospect's business or situation, and points to the need for what you have. Let's say that you're selling food packaging equipment. Your penetrating question could be something like this: "John, in light of the new federal regulations on particulate matter, to what degree does your packaging equipment keep you out of trouble with the government?"

Notice that the question conveyed the impression that you understand his business, and then prompts the prospect to think about the need your product is designed to meet.

All of these things say to the prospect that you are someone apart from the ordinary salesperson — that you understand them. There is little that is more attractive to a person than being understood.

5.   Instead of asking to be called back, leave a message indicating that you will call him/her back at a specific time. So, instead of saying, "Please return my call," you say, " I understand you are not available at the moment. I'll call you at 4:15 this afternoon to pursue this discussion with you."

6.   If you do leave a request for them to call you, make sure that someone is available to take the call and schedule the appointment.

Saying "please return my call," and then going off with your cell phone busy all day is not very smart. When they call, they wind up leaving a voice mail for you. Instead, leave a number of a customer service person (or your spouse, etc.), with times and dates when you are available to make the appointment. Don't frustrate them by having to leave a voice mail for you!

In the next section, I'm going to discuss what to do after you've left several voice mail messages with no return call.

Good luck!

A.4 In this section I'm going to discuss what to do if all of your previous efforts are unsuccessful.

First, a reminder of the perspective from which we should view this problem. It's this – there is no simple, easy solution. I wish I could provide you with a magic phrase or set of "secret" words that are guaranteed to get the prospect to return your call and grant you an audience. But it is just not that easy. Influencing new prospects to return your call and to invest their time in the speculative venture of seeing another salesperson is not a simple thing. And, clearly, it is growing more difficult.

There is a principle that we need to grasp if we're going to be more effective at this most difficult task. The principle is this: There is no short cut, no simple, easy magic answer. There are, however, some principals and strategies that will increase the likelihood of you getting an appointment with the elusive prospect. That means that you are going to have to invest serious planning time and serious creative thought in improving your results.

Okay. You've prepared an effective opening statement, and you've sent a creative pre-call touch. You've made several calls, using the opening statement that you have prepared, and making reference to the pre-call touch that you delivered. You've used some of the tactics that I discussed last month.

But, alas, no return call. What now?

Here are two possibilities.

1. Send them a "why not" fax or email.

This is a document that asks for them to check a line and return it. You offer them a number of responses which provide different reasons why they haven't returned your call. Then, all they need to do is check the one that most accurately applies, and return the fax or email. It helps if your document is light-hearted and humorous in its tone. Here's an example:

John, you're driving me nuts! I've been trying, unsuccessfully, to reach you by phone. Since talking to you is important to me, would you take a moment and check one of the lines below that most accurately describes your position, and return this to me? Thanks.

Dave Kahle

_____ You're calling the wrong person.
Try_____ at extension_____

_____ I'm hard of hearing, and haven't heard any of your voice mail messages. Call me on (date)_____ at (time)_____ and I'll take the call.

_____ I've been extremely busy. But, if you call me on (date)_____. at (time)_____, I'll take the call.

_____ I have absolutely no interest in (saving money) (expanding my business) (saving time), etc. So, don't bother calling again.

_____ I appreciate your tenacity. You really must have something that can benefit me. Call me on (date)_____ at (time)_____ and we'll talk.

It's amazing how a fax like this can change the climate and result in a breakthrough. Thousands of salespeople have used their own version of the "Why Not?" fax with great success.

Here's another option.

2. Meet them outside of the confines of the business. This requires some preparation on your part, and is only effective if the potential payback is worth the time. But, if it's a large potential account, then it may be worth the time and effort. You may need to be creative with this one.

> **A. Find out where they go, and go there.**
>
> > For example, your prospect may be a member of an association or group. Find out when that group meets, and arrange to go to the meeting. There, introduce yourself to the person, establish a bit of a face-to-face relationship, and then refer to that event when you call them the next day.
> >
> > Local and regional trade shows and association meetings are great for this kind of thing. But you may want to extend the idea in a creative fashion. For example, one of my clients sold to attorneys. They are notoriously hard to get to see. So, he made some inquiries, discovered the local tavern that the attorneys liked to frequent on Friday afternoons, and hung around there in order to meet, face to face, his prospects.
>
> **B. Reach them in other out-of-the-normal places.**
>
> > Again, this requires some creativity on your part. At one point in my sales career, I sold to surgeons.

They were almost impossible to see at their offices. However, when they were in the hospital, they had more time and were more amenable to visiting with you. So, I'd find out the surgery schedule of that particular surgeon, arrive in the hospital and have him paged. When he responded to the page, I'd mention that I was in the hospital at the moment, and could he take a few minutes to see me. Almost always the answer was yes.

One of my colleagues even went to this extreme. Before I mention this, let me clearly say that I am not advocating in any way that you do this. Just the opposite. I do not want you to do what my colleague did. I'm only offering it as an example of creatively meeting someone outside of the normal places.

This colleague of mine needed to see a certain department head in a hospital. This key contact would not take his calls, nor return them. He was locked out of any progress in this major account until he could get a face-to-face meeting with her.

So, he got creative. (Once again, understand that I am not advocating you do this.) He waited in the employee parking lot for the shift change, and noted which car she got into to drive home. Then, the next day, he let the air out of one of the tires. When she came out to drive home at the end of her day, he miraculously appeared to help her change the tire. The next day, she took his call.

Where there is a will, there is a way. If the potential of the account is worth it, become creative in how you will attempt to make that first contact.

Chapter Seven ~ Dealing with Voice Mail

Q #19. "In the last telephone seminar, someone asked about getting past the gatekeeper to find the decision-maker. If the name of the decision maker is known, is there any potential pitfall in stating to the gatekeeper, 'This is my name and I am calling for Mr. Johnson,' instead of asking, 'This is my name, is Mr. Johnson available?'"

In response to this question, I asked for ideas from the readers of my E-Zine. I received a number of helpful ideas. I've edited the best of them a bit, and used the person's initials rather than their full name. I hope you enjoy the experiences and insights of some of your colleagues.

A.1 It is my opinion that if you were to say you were calling for Mr. Johnson, then at least the gatekeeper will be of the opinion that Mr. Johnson is expecting you and that you may indeed get through on this premise.

If, however, you ask if Mr. Johnson is available, then the gatekeeper has to call Mr. Johnson to find out, and if Mr. Johnson is a little busy, he is more than likely to say he isn't available - too many choices for Mr. Johnson.

Furthermore, I would like to suggest that if salespeople make appointments, they are more likely to see the person full stop. If you can say to the gatekeeper, "I am here to see Mr. Johnson for our 2:00 pm appointment," then neither the gatekeeper nor Mr. Johnson can turn you away.

In suggesting to our representatives that they make appointments, we have cut down on many a wasted call. We find our customers to be more responsive and our reps to be more prepared.

A.B.

A.2 In response to the question how to get to the decision maker, either of the two suggestions would not make a difference - I have found that however you ask for Mr. Johnson, the chance of getting through is almost zero. However, if you approach the call as "Mary, (assistant's name) this is John Smith. Is Dave (Mr. Johnson's first name) available right now?" tends to work much better. They still may ask you what you are calling for, but if said with confidence and authority, you can get through.

J.P.

A.3 In general, I have found that telling the gatekeeper who you are calling for is more effective than asking if he's available. Every time we ask a question, we leave ourselves open to hearing "no"...and we already get enough of that! Also, people are trained to do what they are told. Most importantly, when we speak to others, we are also speaking to ourselves, and stating that I am calling for the decision-maker reminds me of my purpose, and removes the possibility that I will not get to speak with them. A gatekeeper will hear in my voice that I deserve and expect to be put through. That's why I am calling, and any other outcome would be...well, strange.

With this posture, I have had gatekeepers actually apologize to me if the decision-maker was not available! I want to be clear that I am never pushy or rude. I am well aware that the gatekeeper has the leverage - always. But I do have confidence and credibility. Once you make enough calls in your life, you stop looking for practice, and start going for results.

The only exception to this practice that I can think of is when the receptionist is an amiable, accommodating personality.

This personality style often dislikes saying "no" more than we dislike hearing it, and a lighter touch, giving them the opportunity to be of service, works best with them.

However, when in doubt, remember that we don't ask our purpose...we declare it!

N.L.

A.4 As a gatekeeper of the President of a large corporation, I would say it doesn't make much difference at all. I divert anywhere from 20 to 30 calls per day from our President. The ones that impress me the most (and by the way, that's what it takes), are the ones that give me all the valuable information up-front. Most people call and insist on speaking only to him and the answer that works the best is "he's not here". If they are up-front with me, telling me what they need him for and giving me the information I require to have a discussion with him about it, then it's possible that he may be interested and have me return their call.

Most of the time people are calling for the President and he is not the person that they need to speak with at all. In our company, maybe a CEO, COO, Vice-President, Office Manager, or Sales Manager would be more likely to handle the phone call.

If the person calling explains to me what it is they want, they can usually be referred to someone else that handles whatever it is they are offering.

H.

A.5 I have a thought on the above that has worked for me...

While there are certainly two approaches here, one is a bit more effective (or at least has been for me). You can take the "bull in the china shop" route and attempt to blow-by the gatekeeper in hopes that his/her training was poor and you are not interested in creating a relationship with him/her by simply stating a demand that you are calling for Mr. Johnson. This approach implies that you do not care about the gatekeeper, and that he or she may not even be human.

By using a phone voice that shows you care, not only about getting to your contact, but also through to the gatekeeper, you have created an "open-door" for future phone calls. By establishing rapport with the gatekeeper up front, your tone of voice, the questions you ask, and the manner in which you ask those questions, makes all the difference in the world in gaining the opportunity to meet with your contact and create a mutually beneficial partnership.

J.E.

A.6 The age old "Getting past the gatekeeper!"

How about this: Just like you would do with the decision maker, you need to establish a rapport (relationship) with the gatekeeper. The first call will let you know if he/she is tough or not. Ask for her name. Next call might go something like this:

- ABC Manufacturing, Can I help you?

- Hi, is this Betty?

- Yes, this is Betty.

- Hi Betty, this is Joe from XYZ Magazine, how are you today?

- Fine Joe, how are you?

- I'm great. I was looking for John, is he in today?

- What is this in regards to?

- Well Betty, I wanted to visit with John on the phone a couple of minutes. We have some great advertising opportunities available and thought John would be interested in hearing from me. You told me last time I called that he was the person in charge of marketing and advertising for your company.

Gatekeepers are people too! Talk to them that way! Put a smile on someone's face today.

R. V.

A.7 With regards to the gatekeeper question, I would suggest be less formal, act as if you know Bill instead of Mr. Johnson. "Hey is Bill around? Tell him Keith is calling." I find that works for me.

K.H.

A.8 Here are some tips from when I worked as a gatekeeper: At some companies, the relief staff is not as efficient at gate keeping, so try to call during lunch and coffee breaks. You might get through. If you sound like you know the person you are trying to reach, you have a better chance that the gatekeeper will announce your call (instead of politely informing you that your target is not available at the moment and offering to take a message).

L.B.

8

ASKING GOOD
SALES QUESTIONS

Your Most Powerful Sales Tool

Did you enjoy what you had for dinner last night?

You are probably wondering what that question has to do with sales. Bear with me a moment, and answer the question.

Now, pause a moment, and think about what you did when you read that question. Your mind probably flashed back to yesterday evening, and you saw a picture in your mind's eye of what you had for dinner. Then you recalled your response to the dinner, and made a judgment that you did or didn't enjoy it.

Here's the point. I was able to direct your thinking by asking you a question. You thought about what I wanted you to think about, and you thought about it in the way I wanted. That's an illustration of the power of a question. It directs an individual's thinking.

> *A well-phrased, appropriately timed question is your most powerful sales tool.*

That's what makes asking a good question the single most effective thing you can do with a customer. A well-phrased, appropriately-timed question is your most powerful sales tool.

Here's what good questions will do for you.

1. Good questions direct your customer's thinking.

When you use a good question, or a series of good questions, you penetrate your prospect's mind and direct his/her thinking.

There is something in human beings that makes it almost impossible not to think of the answer when we are asked a question. I'm not sure whether it's something genetic, or whether we're conditioned from birth to always think of the answer to a question. Here's an illustration. I'll ask you a question, but I want you to *not* think of the answer. How old are you? If you're like most of us, you thought of the answer, even after I indicated you shouldn't.

Now, consider where the decision to buy your products or services takes place. It happens in the mind of your customer. A good question from you helps focus and shape the direction in which your customer's mind works.

For example, suppose you're shopping for a new car. The salesperson asks you, "Which is more important to you, good fuel economy, or quick pickup?" Until asked, you haven't really thought of it that way. The salesperson's question helps you understand what you really think, and directs your mind along a certain course. Now that you're thinking along that line, the conversation naturally proceeds based on the first answer.

Similarly, you perform a service for your customers when you ask them good questions. Your questions direct their minds along certain paths, and help them clarify their thinking.

2. A good question is your best means of collecting the information that will help you construct a sale.

How do you know what a customer thinks, or what his/her situation is, unless you ask a question? If you're selling a new surgical glove, for example, you first ask questions to discover the surgeon's concerns so that you are able to point out the specific features of the glove that meet those needs. Without first asking questions, you're reduced to working on assumptions about the needs and interests of your customers.

You will do a far better job of selling your products and services if you first use good questions to understand your customer's needs and interests. Good questions help you to see into the mind and heart of your customers, and equip you with the knowledge necessary to make the sale.

3. Good questions build relationships.

The art of asking good questions shows that you care about the person and his/her problems. The more questions you ask about your customer, the more he/she feels your interest.

The law of reciprocity indicates that the more interest you show in a customer, the more likely that customer will be interested in you.

Did you ever attend a reception or cocktail party, and meet someone who was very interested in you? Asked you question after question about yourself? When you parted, you thought to yourself, "What a great person." Why did you think that? Because of what he/she said? Probably not. You thought the person was wonderful because he/she expressed interest in you! And you formed that impression because of the questions they asked of you.

You can make use of this principle by asking good personal questions of your customers and thereby building strong relationships.

4. Good questions convey the perception of your competence.

In other words, your customer sees you as competent and trustworthy — not necessarily by what you say — but rather by what you ask.

Here's an illustration. Suppose you have a problem with your car. You take it into the mechanic down the street and say to him, "My car is making a funny sound." He says to you, "Okay, leave it here and pick it up at five."

You're not reassured by his approach, so you take it to the mechanic across the street. You say the same thing to him. And he says to you, "What kind of sound?" You reply, "A strange thumping sound." And he says "Is it coming from the front or the back of the car?" And you say, "It's coming from the front." And he asks, "Is it a metallic kind of sound or a rubber kind of sound?" You reply, "It's definitely metallic." And he says, "Does it go faster when you go faster and slower when you go slower, or is it the same speed all the time?" You respond, "It definitely speeds up as I do." Then he says, "Okay, leave it here and pick it up at five."

Which mechanic seems to be the more competent? That's easy. Obviously, the one who asked more questions.

Got the idea? The focus and precision of your questions does more to give your customer the perception of your competence than anything else.

Every one of your customers wants to feel that the salesperson he/she is dealing with is competent. You convey that perception by asking good questions about the details of your customers' needs and applications.

Mastering the use of good questions — the salesperson's single most powerful interpersonal tool — in every aspect of your sales interactions will dramatically improve your results.

Q #20. In the seminar, you stated "Anything else?" as one of your 'really good sales questions'. I see it as a close-ended question. Is "What else can I do?" as effective, or more or less effective?

A. What a great question. Let me applaud you for thinking this deeply about the language in the questions that you use. This "thinking about it before you do it" is one of my key commandments for success in sales. And this kind of thoughtful discussion brings out the best in all of us.

I'm sticking with "Anything else?" as a "Really Good Sales Question." Yes, it is a close-ended question, but that doesn't make it bad. There is a time and place for close-ended questions. Remember, "Anything else?" is always used to follow up on some piece of information the customer has given you. Typically, it follows an open-ended question, as in, "Tell me what you look for in a vendor."

When you ask "Anything else?" you generally get one of two answers: Either some more explanation or information from the customer, or the answer, "no." Either of those two answers is good. More explanation gives you more information, and that's good. "No" tells you there is no more, that you have acquired all the pertinent information, and that's good.

The real difference between "Anything else?" and "What else can I do?" is the purpose to the question. "Anything else?" solicits information, and can be used in a broader set of circumstances. See the example above. "What else can I do?" is a more specific question, probing deeper into a more narrow range of possibilities. For example, you couldn't use "What else can I do?" to follow up on the "Tell me what you look for in a vendor" lead.

There is also an implied commitment to the "What else can I do?" question. The implication is that you will do what he/she asks you to. Since you are asking, "What else can I do," it implies that you are willing and able to do more. And that may not be the case. Asking this question may force you into the uncomfortable position of saying "No" to the customer. For example, suppose you say, "What else can I do?" and the customer says, "Drop your price by 10% and deliver twice a week." You know you can't do that, so you say, "I can't do that..." thereby interjecting a negative into the conversation. I think you would have been better off not bringing it up.

9

CRITICAL THINKING

Think A Lot

If you're like a number of other distributors, you're having a good year. The economy is up, business is good, and you're personal sales are probably pretty good. With all that positive news there's a great temptation to coast for a while, to relax and enjoy the status quo.

Unfortunately, that's a luxury you can no longer afford. There was a time, just a few years ago, when you could relax and enjoy the fruits of your labors. You had reached a point where life became easy, your customers were buying from you consistently, and you had your job figured out.

That's no longer advisable. Pressures are growing on your company to reduce their costs and become more productive. The study published by the Distribution Research and Education Foundation, which predicted trends for the distribution industry in the near future, made this prediction:

> *"...panelists believe there will need to be approximately a ten percent decrease in sales and marketing costs as a percentage of sales if acceptable profitability levels are to be maintained...and all of this "cutting" would have to*

*be done during a period when sales and marketing activity
needs to be improved if the company hopes to stay even
or progress."* pg. 189

That means that you, personally, must become far more productive than you've ever been expected to be in the past. Today's performance, no matter how good, will not be sufficient tomorrow.

And that means that you must "Think a Lot." I'm not suggesting that you spend your time day dreaming. Nor am I encouraging you to ponder the meaning of the universe, do a crossword puzzle or memorize the birth dates of all your relatives. All of those exercises would represent ways to think a lot, but they are not the kind of thinking I'm advocating.

Rather, I'm encouraging you to invest your greatest single resource, your mind, in focusing your mental energy on specific portions of your job. That means thinking about certain things, thinking in certain ways, and doing a lot of it.

It's easy to do your job by mindlessly going through the motions. You see the customers with whom you are comfortable, quote the products they ask you about, grumble about the paperwork, and complain about price competition.

That's easy. Unfortunately, it's also a prescription for eventual failure. The world is changing too rapidly today to do your job "mindlessly." Your customers are changing, products and vendors are changing and adapting, and new competitors and technologies are springing up. If you go through your job mindlessly, you'll soon be outdated and ineffectual.

> *That means thinking about certain things,
> thinking in certain ways, and doing a lot of that.*

So, on one hand you have the need to improve your productivity to keep up with the pressures on your company, and on the other, you have the temptation to get into a rut, and go about your job "mindlessly."

The most effective strategy to battle these double temptations is to "Think A Lot."

What should you think about? Here are three of the most important things.

1. Think about your customers.

Ask yourself a series of questions about your customers. As you develop the answers, write them down in your account folders, and repeat the process a few months later. Here are some questions to get you thinking:

- What's changing for this customer?

- What do they want to accomplish this year?

- What can I do to help them meet their goals?

- What is the competition doing in this account?

- What progress have I made in the past few months?

- What can I do now to increase my sales in this account?

Thinking about these questions keeps you constantly close to the changing conditions in your accounts, and keeps you insulated from the tendency to get "mindless."

2. Think about each sales call.

Your face-to-face contact with your customer is the one part of your job that sets you apart from everyone else in your company. It is that aspect of what you do by which you bring value to your company.

If you honestly think about it, you'll probably observe that everything else you do can be done by other people in your company. Someone else can accept orders, train end users, check on back-orders, etc. The only thing you do that no one else in your company does is call on your customers face-to-face. So, your eyeball-to-eyeball interactions with your customers are probably the most important part of your job.

Yet, most observers estimate that the average salesperson spends only about 30% of his time face-to-face with his customers.

Put those two facts together, and you have the sobering conclusion that you spend very little of your time doing that thing that is the most important aspect of your job.

That being the case, doesn't it stand to reason that you ought to invest some time and energy planning for those rare moments when you're face-to-face with your customers?

Ask yourself these questions, and think about the answers, before every sales call:

- What do I want to accomplish?

- What forces are working on my customer that may influence his behavior today?

- What value am I bringing him today?

- Exactly what am I going to ask, say, or communicate?

- What can I do to understand him better?

- What can I do to deepen the relationship?

Going through this disciplined approach to "thinking about your sales calls" will be the single most effective thing you can do to improve your productivity.

3. Think about continuously improving yourself.

First, commit yourself to the challenge of continuous improvement. Be discontent with the level of proficiency you have obtained. Be discontent with your results. Think about everything you do and examine ways to improve and wring more value out of it.

Challenge and question everything you do. Is this the best way to write up a quote? Should you be visiting this account, or would the other one hold more potential? Should you really be spending your time promoting this product, or is another one more important? Should you really be lunching with this customer or should you invest that time in another? Is this the best way to file your old quotes, keep track of customer contacts, and file product literature?

It was during one of these introspective "continuous improvement" thinking sessions, that I developed one of the strategies that proved most effective for me. Early in my tenure as a distribution salesperson, my manager told me that most salespeople don't make it a point to present a product or product line at each sales call. So he encouraged me to always have a product or product line to present on every sales call. I thought he knew more than I did, so I followed his advice.

And then the thought occurred to me, as I was questioning everything that I did, that if it was a good idea to present one product, it may be twice as good an idea to offer two or more.

By doing so, I could multiply the number of sales presentations I made in roughly the same amount of face-to-face sales time. It was a way of improving the quality of my sales time by increasing the quantity of sales presentations. From then on, I made it a point to have several items or products to present on every sales call. That's just one example.

Got the idea? Never rest. Be discontent with every aspect of your job in order to provide the stimulation to improve on it. Question everything. Think a lot.

It'll be your key to continuous, life-long improvement.

Q #21. When we get through to the person we want to talk to, we most often hear that they are happy with their current supplier. How can we overcome that?

A. You are encountering the classic B2B prospect put-off. There are a number of ways to deal with this. Here's one. Let's recognize that the conversation seems to be centered on the wrong issues. When you call for an appointment, the issue is not whether that company should buy from you. The issue is whether or not the person on the other end of the phone should invest 15 – 30 minutes of time with you. You should be selling the appointment, not your company. In other words, focus on giving them a reason to *see* you. The reason to *buy* from you will come later.

Think about these questions before you call:

Why should someone spend 15 minutes or so with you?

What are they going to learn?

What will that investment of time do for them?

Let's create a scenario and work through this. Let's say that you manage to get the person you want to talk with on the phone. You give your short intro pitch, and ask for an appointment. Your prospect says, *"We're happy with our current supplier."*

You say, *"I appreciate that, and I in no way expect that you'll change that. There may come a time when your current supplier can't deliver, or perhaps isn't able to meet your changing requirements in some other way. In that case, it would be helpful for you if you had a relationship with an alternate supplier. I'm suggesting that you invest just 15 to 20 minutes with me so that you'll have the knowledge you'll need to avoid a potential crises some time in the future. I'll be in your area Monday and Tuesday of next week. Which of those work better for you?"*

Let's examine what you did. You changed the focus of the conversation. It's no longer about his relationship with his current suppliers. It is about how he would be wise to invest some time with you. You are not selling your company, you are selling the appointment.

Then you gave him a reason to see you – some benefit that the prospect will gain from the appointment. You didn't threaten the current relationship in any way. Then you immediately asked for the appointment again.

That's one way to deal with this extremely common objection.

Q #22. *What can I expect when I work up the line of executives when the key contact is holding us back from selling beyond occasional orders?*

A. First, remember the context in which this discussion took place – how to protect a good account from the competition. As you recall from the program, a good account is one in which you have the lion's share of the account's market. So, the situation described above – only occasional orders – would not be a good account!

However, that doesn't mean that you can't pursue the strategy of working up the line to meet your key contact's boss. It does mean that you may not be successful at it.

The best way to attempt this is to ask your key contact to introduce you. Give him/her a reason why you need to meet his/her boss, and ask for their help. You are not necessarily going to bypass your key contact and sell to the boss. Rather, you are making sure that you have access to and awareness of the boss when you need it.

10

MANAGING INFORMATION

"I'm spending more and more time dealing with information. It's squeezing out my selling time."

Welcome to the Information Age. You are not unique. This problem of information inundation is a relatively new, but almost universal, threat to your livelihood. Four or five years ago, salespeople were not too concerned with it. Today, dealing with information is so critical that it is an important part of almost every seminar I present.

Here's the issue. Technological advances in recent years have multiplied the amount of information that you must handle. The quantity of information landing on your lap has increased from sources all around you. Think about how much information you must keep about your customers. A few years ago, it was okay to keep everything in your head. Today you need forms, documents, files and systems, both electronic and paper, to keep it all straight. Consider the technical details of the products and programs you sell. Aren't they more complex and sophisticated than just a few years ago? And all that complexity takes the form of additional information that you must organize and master.

What about the computer systems you use and the information produced by them? Most salespeople I know could spend eight to twelve hours a week just reviewing computer printouts if they so choose. Add in memos from the boss, service bulletins, price increases, government regulations, new product specifications, the details of ever more complicated applications, etc., and your job is awash in information.

The sheer volume of information coming at you is like an approaching tidal wave. If you don't create some safe haven for yourself, you're going to be rendered ineffective by the absolute mass of information.

Imagine how many precious selling hours you could waste each week if you don't harness that tidal wave of information. Or, imagine the time robbed from your family and personal life by the time it takes to handle more and more stuff.

> *The sheer volume of information coming at you is like an approaching tidal wave. If you don't create some safe haven for yourself, you're going to be rendered ineffective by the absolute mass of information.*

It's time to recognize the problem for what it is: A serious and malevolent new threat to your effectiveness.

So, what do you do? How do you overcome this threat? How do you get control over the flow of information and protect your valuable selling time?

Defend yourself!

One strategy is to become defensive. In other words, to develop ways to defend yourself from being overcome with useless information. The idea is to keep tempting but useless information from stealing your time.

To do so, you need to understand and implement two key processes. The first is "screening." Imagine the screen on your window. This fine mesh allows those breezes that you want to flow into the house, while it keeps out of the house those insects that you don't want. So, it allows in that which you want, and keeps out that which you don't want.

That's the idea behind the process of screening – allowing in that which you want, and keeping out that which you don't want. Unfortunately, you can't surround yourself with a physical screen. But you can implement the discipline of "screening" all the information that comes your way. To do so, you need to establish the habit of quickly assessing every piece of information that cries out for your time and to quickly decide if it is likely to be useful. *Useful* is the key and operative word.

If your quick perusal of a piece of information leads you to believe that it may be *useful,* you let that piece in. If you believe it will not be *useful*, you keep it out. In other words, you dispose of it.

Let's imagine a scenario. You've come into the office and pulled a pile of stuff out of your mailbox. The first thing you see is a new price list for a product line you rarely sell. Is this *useful* to you? Probably not. You throw it out. Next is a service bulletin on a piece of equipment that you haven't sold in years. Is it *useful?* Probably not. Out it goes. Next is a computer report comparing last year's sales in three product lines to the sales from two years ago on those same lines. Is it *useful?* In the round file it goes.

Finally, there's a memo from the boss outlining the agendas, location and schedules of sales meetings for the next two months. Better hold on to that one. You continue on this way, quickly appraising every piece of information, and disposing of every piece you deem to be not *useful*.

This whole process may have only taken a few seconds. But your disciplined "screening" process kept a lot of "useless" information from sucking away your time. The net effect was that you created more selling time for yourself by disciplining yourself to keep out that which is useless, and to allow in that which is useful.

Now you have a pile of stuff which, on first glance, looked like it might be useful. Now what do you do? Implement the second key process – *triaging*. You may be familiar with the word. It has a medical origin. In every hospital emergency room, there is someone who performs the 'triaging' function. They make a quick assessment of the condition of the incoming patients, and then send them to different degrees and types of treatment depending on that initial assessment. So, one person is told to wait in the waiting room for a while longer, another is sent directly to the OB department, yet another is admitted to surgery, etc. The person who does the triaging sends each patient to a location for treatment based on that initial assessment.

That's what you do with the pile of information on your desk. You look at each piece of information, and send it to the location where it can be dealt with appropriately. So, for example, you have a spot for "Read and handle immediately." You have a file for "Put this stuff into my account folders." You have a folder for "Study this when you have time." You have yet another labeled "File with product information."

Now that you know what your options are, you are ready to 'triage' the pile of information on your desk. Look at each piece, and place it in the location where you can deal with it appropriately. If you have thought about this before hand and arranged an effective file system, this process may take you a just a few moments. At the end of that time, you have everything in its place and you can now deal with it in the time and place you choose. You sit down with the "Read and handle immediately" pile and process that.

The "study this when you have time" file goes in your briefcase to be reviewed while you are waiting for appointments, or on those occasions when you are having lunch by yourself. The stuff for "account folders" and "product folders" goes home with you and is reviewed and filed in your home office all at once on Friday afternoons or Saturday mornings.

By implementing these two disciplines, you've taken what could have been an hour or two of information-engagement and turned it into a few moments of disciplined involvement on your part. You've gotten back hours of selling time, and not allowed the tidal wave of information to wash you away.

This process of *screening* and *triaging* can work for you with any kind of information. Apply it to your list of daily emails and email attachments. Ditto the stuff in your inbox, and the pile of envelopes and catalogues that appear every day in the mail. Do the same with your choice of Internet surfing and TV channel hopping.

Unfortunately, the information-rich world in which we live has created a situation where some of the techniques and strategies that used to work for you are no longer as effective as they once were. To maintain your effectiveness in a rapidly changing world, you need to take on new skills and processes. Defending yourself from the tidal wave of information which threatens to drown you is one of them.

Q #23. In your recent phone seminar on handling objections, you talked about using "Proof" like letters of recommendation and testimonials. How do you get them?

A. The short answer is that you ask for them. That's overly simple, however. It's a bit more complicated than that. First, make sure that your customers are satisfied with the product or service you sold them. So, shortly after experiencing your product, call for an appointment and visit the customer. Ask them if the product or service did what was expected. Find out how well they like it, and what impact they are seeing on their business. Take notes during this time, and write down, word-for-word, the comments that your customers make.

Assuming your customers are happy with what you sold them, ask, "If I could make it very easy for you to write a little letter of recommendation, would you?" If you hear a yes, then offer to write the letter, using the customer's words (which you have noted), and deliver it to them. All your customers have to do is sign it and give it back to you.

Borrow a couple pieces of letterhead, write the letter as if it were from the customer, using the words that you collected, and bring it back to the customer. He signs it, and bingo, you have a letter of recommendation.

There is an additional fringe benefit. You also gain some additional currency with the original customer, who is flattered that you asked him/her to write the letter.

Do this a few times, and before long you'll have a folder full of "proof."

Q #24. I've heard you mention several times the importance of prioritizing and targeting customers. Can you shed some more light on this?

A. This is a key issue with me, as I believe it is one of the ways to make the biggest, most rapid change in your results. Too much good quality sales time and talent is squandered on customers who aren't worth the investment. If I can help salespeople adjust their investment in time so that they are spending more time on the high potential customers and less time on others, they'll see an almost immediate improvement in results.

So, I have developed, over years of trial and error, a simple but incredibly powerful system for prioritizing and targeting accounts. While I don't have space here to describe the whole system, I can suggest several things you can do to institute this practice in your sales team.

1. Set up some company-wide definitions. Everyone should understand what an "A" account is. Likewise for "B" and "C" accounts. In addition, there ought to be some standards for how you define each of these. For example, you might say an "A" account is one who could buy $1,000,000 of your product each year. So how do you determine that an account could buy $1,000,000? Do you guess? Or do you use some more sophisticated means of coming to that number? You need to answer these kinds of questions.

2. Once you've created the criteria and definitions, train the entire group in the use of those concepts. Require that, by a certain date, they have analyzed and rated all of their customers. You may even develop some forms, electronic or hard copy, which everyone uses.

3. Now, legislate that everyone should spend the biggest portion of their time with the "A" accounts. My rule is 50% of your time with the "A" accounts, and 50% of your time with everyone else.

4. Manage the implementation. Every time you ride with a salesperson, discuss it and look for evidence that indicates the salesperson is following through on using the system. Make it an issue in sales meetings and in evaluations.

I have developed a variety of resources to help you with this. The system is described in detail in my book, <u>10 Secrets of Time Management for Salespeople</u>. It's also dealt with in the time management addendum to <u>How to Excel at Distributor Sales</u>.

The reason I have so much material on this subject is that I believe that it is one of the key behaviors for sales success. Everyone should be using it.

Q #25. Can you direct me to resources that give me information on using current technology to utilize when calling on my accounts to cover my sales territory? What I am most interested in is the new usage of GPS systems, wireless contact management systems, and this sort of technology that is available but not being used by the masses of salespeople or sales managers. I want to integrate a mobile sales function utilizing current available technology.

A. The best source I know of is *Sales & Marketing Management* magazine. You know that this area is changing daily, and SMM is very current with articles and advertisements that can guide you to the up-to-date material. Get the magazine, and review it for vendors, websites, and associations that will take you where you want to go.

11

BRINGING THE
CUSTOMER VALUE

The Value-Added Sales Call

"My customers seem to have less time available for me than before. They are harder to see, and when I do get in front of them, they often seem rushed or preoccupied. What can I do about this?"

Sound familiar? It's a question that I am hearing more and more often. I'm sure you have run it through your mind a few times.

It may be that the problem is you. You may be irritating and abrasive, and over time your customers may have decided that they don't want you around.

But it's probably not you. It's your customer. No matter what you sell, it is likely that your customer has more to do and less time in which to do it than ever before. Your customer's lack of time is a relatively recent phenomenon. It wasn't much of an issue a few years ago, but it has become universal and growing in intensity day by day. Your customer is overworked and pressed for time. As a result, there is just not enough time in the day to get everything done. Some things have to go. A long, leisurely conversation with a salesperson is often one of those things that is going.

I believe we are the beginning of a new trend – a trend with awesome implications for salespeople. It used to be that being viewed as a "value-added" vendor was a desirable position to occupy in the customer's mind. That meant that the product or service you represented brought your customer more value for the money than the offerings of your competitors. It was why they did business with you.

Notice the focus was on the product or service you represented. The process involved – the sales calls you made on the customer, and the discussions you had with him or her – were viewed as a means to an end. It was what both of you did in order to come to the exchange of money for your value-added offerings.

> *Today, not only must the product or service bring value to the customer, but the time you spend with the customer must also be of value to him or her.*

Those were the rules, and customers and salespeople understood them. These rules of sales interactions are deeply ingrained – so deeply, in fact, that many of us cannot conceive of the profession of sales being done any other way. It is what we know, and how we have made our living.

But the rules are changing. We are at the beginning of a new paradigm for the field salesperson. The new paradigm is this: *Today, not only must the product or service bring value to the customer, but the time you spend with the customer must also be of value to him or her.* In other words, the sales process itself must bring value to your customer. Your customer must gain something from every sales call. He/she must see a reason for spending time with you – a payback for his investment of time.

Now, of course you have your agenda, and you have your objectives for the sales call. You know what value you want to gain from the meeting with your customer. But what about your customer? What is he going to gain from investing that precious 30 – 45 minutes with you?

In today's time-compressed and overwhelming world, your sales call must bring the customer some value. Here's a way to visualize this emerging new rule. Suppose you were to make a routine sales call on a regular customer. At the end of the call you said, "Okay, John, that will be $150.00." In other words, you charge him for the value he received by talking with you. Would he pay your bill? Would he have derived enough value from the time he spent with you so that he would gladly pay you for it?

Okay, the illustration may seem a bit over the edge. Most industries are not at the point, yet, where they will charge for sales calls. But in the information rich, too-many-things-to-do world in which you and your customers live, time is more precious than money.

When you ask for your customer's time, you are asking for something very limited and very precious. If you take 30 minutes of his day, he has invested 6.25% of his workday in you. He has a thousand other things he could have done in that time. What did he get for that investment with you?

The point is this: If you are going to be successful in the Information Age economy, you must focus on bringing something of value to your customers every time you ask them to invest their time in you. You must view every sales call through the perspective of the value you can bring to your customers. A sales call is no longer just about the objectives that you want to achieve, it is also about the objectives your customers want to achieve. It's as if you present that $150.00 bill at the end of every sales call and expect to be paid.

So, how can you adjust to new situation? Here are some proven practices that will help you make the transition:

1. Understand your customer's situation as thoroughly as possible before you take his time.

Your customer expects you to know something about his business, his customers, his processes and his problems before you visit. That means that you must spend more time before a sales call gathering information about that customer. Check to see if the customer has a website, and gather useful information from it. Call and ask the receptionist to send you a company brochure. Ask around your company to see what other colleagues might know about the account.

2. Think through the sales call from the customer's perspective.

Put yourself in the shoes of that customer. What else does he/she have to do other than talk to you? What problems is he facing, what opportunities? How can you bring him or her something that will simplify his job, help him overcome his problems, or reduce the amount of time he spends on your project?

3. Prepare something of potential value for every call.

This is a long-range strategy. As you consistently hold to this strategy, over time you'll build up a certain expectation in the customer's mind. Don't expect an immediate payback from this strategy, but, nonetheless, stick to it for the long haul.

Try to bring something to every sales call that your customer would think is valuable. This can, of course, be your latest and greatest product or service, providing that it really would help them. Or, it may be an idea that you have found for a change in their processes, or it may be a new way to implement something they have purchased from you in the past. Maybe it's a copy of an article that you thought might help them. It can even be a good question you share with them that gets them thinking about their business in a different way.

After a few such calls, your customer will come to respect you and look forward to your calls, knowing that you're not there just to work some agenda of yours, but rather he'll come to expect to gain something from your sales calls.

You'll find it easier to make appointments and get time with your customers when you've built in them the expectation that the time spent with you will be well worth the cost of it.

If you are guided by this principle of always bringing something of value, you'll recognize that there is another side to this coin. If you have nothing to leave the customer that will be of value to that customer, you probably shouldn't make the sales call. Don't take his time.

4. Be a resource.

One of my clients suggested that salespeople need to be the "customer's search engine." I couldn't agree more. Strive to be the customer's most trusted and most knowledgeable resource, the customer's source of information, not just about your product, but about the whole category of things that you sell, their applications, and their advantages and problems.

Share information that is bigger than just the product or service that you sell. If you do, then your customer will look forward to your visits and view them as valuable.

I realize that this is a change in thinking for a lot of sales reps. But it's a change that is coming, whether you want to make it or not. Your choice is to be a leader and thus gain a significant edge over your competition, or to wait until the market forces you to change. The choice is yours.

Q #26. How much time should you expect from a customer for an appointment?

A. This is one of those many questions for which the answer always begins with "It depends." It depends, first of all, if this is a prospect (someone who has not purchased) or a regular customer (someone who buys regularly). Generally speaking, you can expect more time with a customer than with a prospect.

It depends, secondly, on the understanding your customer has about the purpose and agenda of the call. For example, if you asked for 60 minutes in order to detail your response to his request for a proposal or a piece of equipment, then you should expect 60 minutes. If you asked for a short period of time to introduce you and your company, then you are probably lucky to get 30 minutes.

It depends, next, on your personal reputation. If you are a seasoned rep who, over the years, has built a reputation that you won't waste your customer's time, and that you are always prepared to share something you think will be of value to the customer, then you should expect more time. If, however, you don't have such a reputation with the customer, then you should expect less time.

It depends, finally, on your objective for the sales call. If you want to check up on the delivery of an order, for example, it probably shouldn't take you more than ten minutes. If you want to get a tour of the facility and meet four of the key people, it could take a couple of hours.

As an overall rule to guide you, the call shouldn't take any longer than it needs to. Of equal importance to how much time you think the call should take is how much time the customer has to devote to it. As you know, time is the scarce commodity of our age, and your customer doesn't have much of it. You need to respect your customer's time constraints. If you ask for an hour of your customer's time, that's 16% of his day. Are you that important? Will you bring him/her enough value to justify that? Never allow your preconceived notions to override your customer's time constraints.

To read more about this go to www.davekahle.com/article/constraints.htm and read my article, "Dealing With Your Customer's Time Constraints."

Q #27. Sales are down, operating expenses are up, and management is crying that sales expenses are up. What should a salesperson do in such a situation?

A. These certainly are challenging times. I've been through enough of these to have learned some things. Even though I never liked going through difficult times, and would not wish them on anyone, I can honestly say that I always came out of them stronger, more confident, with more capabilities and more security than ever. You can, too.

Here are a few things that I have learned along the way. I know this is easier said than done, but don't worry about things you cannot control. You cannot single-handedly change the economic climate, nor can you single-handedly control your company's response to a difficult economy. The time, effort and emotional energy you expend fretting over what might happen is wasted. The economy is going to do what it is going to do regardless of your efforts. So, don't waste time worrying about it.

Instead, concentrate on what you can do, on the things that you can control. You can control your attitude, and you can control your behavior.

Work on keeping your attitude positive. A positive attitude for a salesperson is more than just a warm and fuzzy thing. It has very real, practical value. When you have a positive attitude, you look for opportunities and good things to happen. Since you are expecting them and looking for them, you see them. If your attitude is negative and pessimistic, you don't expect opportunities to present themselves. Since you don't expect them, you don't see them when they develop. As a result, you pass over opportunities, and your negative attitude becomes a self-fulfilling prophecy.

165

In addition to attending to your attitude, you can control your behavior. Focus on doing your job more effectively. Make sure you are digging deeper in your good accounts and finding additional opportunities to expand the business. Get a good sales book to read, and try to implement some of the ideas. (My book, *10 Secrets of Time Management for Salespeople,* would be a great place to start.)

Now is also the time to be very sensitive to what your competitors are doing. They may be cutting back on their service or reducing their workforce, and those actions may open up opportunities for you. Discipline yourself to make a certain number of cold calls on prospect accounts each week. There is nothing like new people, new situations, and new opportunities to energize you.

Pay attention to your personal financial situation. Now is not the time to make big purchases on your credit card. Now is also not the time to sign contracts, enter into long term leases, etc. All of those turn into monthly obligations, and in times of uncertainty, monthly obligations multiply your stress and reduce your options.

Here's one more that may surprise you.

Exercise. Put yourself on a disciplined exercise program. Exercise is one of only a handful of practices that have been proven to reduce stress for salespeople. You'll feel better, have more energy and less stress, think clearer and be more emotionally stable if you exercise regularly.

It really is the difficult times that shape your character and define your success. Anyone can do well when the market is growing all around you. It takes a true professional to survive and thrive in time of adversity.

12

STAYING MOTIVATED

Staying Motivated In Challenging Times

One of my Ezine subscribers recently sent me this question:

"I really struggle with the highs and lows of field sales. Most days I feel like the weight of the world is on my shoulders. In this economy, especially, it's difficult to stay positive. Any suggestions?"

This is one of those rarely voiced issues that every salesperson must confront sooner or later. Sales is an emotional roller coaster, and unless you figure out how to manage those emotions and keep yourself motivated, you'll have a difficult time succeeding.

This is particularly true right now. As I write this, the economy continues to struggle, and unemployment is higher than it has been for years. Many companies are cutting back, there are fewer jobs available, and pressures to perform are greater than ever.

I can emphasize with the anxiety felt by the reader. It's easy to lose our motivation.

However, even though the world around us may be dreary and depressing, that in no way reduces our personal need to do the best we can. And that means that we all have a responsibility to stay motivated.

It is amazing what a difference a few degrees of attitude adjustment can make in our performance. Try this little exercise. Tell yourself these things: *"Business is terrible. All of my customers are struggling. Nobody wants to see me, and when they do, it's just to complain."* Now wallow in those thoughts for a moment, and note how much energy and enthusiasm you have.

Now, think the opposite: *"I have great opportunities. My customers need me more today than ever. I have valuable solutions for them. It's a great time to have this job."* Roll those around in your mind for a while. Note how much energy and enthusiasm you have.

As you reflect on this exercise, it's clear that your energy, enthusiasm and drive to succeed come as a result of your thoughts. And here is one of the most powerful truths known to mankind: You can control your thoughts.

Succeeding in difficult times depends a great deal on our motivation. Staying motivated requires us to take charge of our thoughts.

> **And here is one of the most powerful truths known to mankind: You can control your thoughts.**

I've heard dozens of salespeople say, "I've tried positive thinking. It just isn't me." I agree that it is difficult to patch a bunch of positive thoughts on top of an essentially negative personality. The issue is deeper than that. Let's, therefore, examine the deeper issues.

At the heart of motivation lies a pair of powerful beliefs which you must embrace if you are going to successfully motivate yourself. Without a wholehearted commitment to these foundational beliefs, all the techniques and tactics for self-motivation are like spreading wallpaper over crumbling plaster. It may hold temporarily, but it is soon going to deteriorate into a mess.

Here's the first foundational principle. **You must believe that you can do better than you are now doing.** The second is this: **You must accept that it is your responsibility to do so.**

Sounds so simple and common sense. However, the more I observe people, and salespeople specifically, the more convinced I am that the majority of people do not share these core beliefs. Rather, they are in the habit of making excuses for their situation. Or, they believe that it's really fate that determines their success, not their actions. Or, they believe that success is for someone else, not them. They never really grab onto the first of these foundational principles.

Others believe that they can achieve greater degrees of success. They embrace the idea, intellectually. They accept the first principle, but they never internalize the second. They become content with their situation, no matter what it is, and remain in pre-established comfort zones. Or they look at their manager as the person who is responsible for their success, or lack thereof. Or, it's their parent's fault, or their spouse's, or... the list goes on.

Whether you are struggling with a lack of energy that accompanies a bad day, or you're depressed and frustrated with your lack of progress on a larger scale, the first thing to do is to examine your core beliefs. If you really accept these two principles, you have the keystone in place to become highly motivated.

Having said that, there are some specific techniques that you can use to keep yourself motivated day-to-day. Here are a couple proven techniques.

1. Have something you are working to accomplish.

This can be an important and compelling goal like saving enough money for a down payment on a house. When you are working toward something like that, your emotions of the moment have a tendency to be lower priority than your drive to achieve. If you are trying to make money for a home for your family, so what if you're tired or depressed? Get out and do it.

The same thing is true of a compelling purpose. I believe that every salesperson should have a clear articulation of his/her purpose in life. I once began a ten-week sales training program with a requirement that everyone write a two-sentence "life purpose" statement.

Why is that? Because it gives power and focus to everything you do. In the job of the salesperson, there will be lots of times when you find it to be difficult, when things don't go your way. You may lose a big deal, or be unable to get anyone to return your calls. At times like those, it sure helps to view them within the context of a larger perspective – a life purpose.

By the way, I've run across a book that helps you with this project. I've put it in the "Recommended Resources" portion of my web site. Check out *The Purpose Driven Life* by Rick Warren.

2. Proactively put positive thoughts into your mind.

Make a point of taking charge of your mind and the kind of thoughts you choose to think. For ages, wise and thoughtful people have discovered an extremely powerful principle:

Your actions arise from your thoughts, and you can choose your thoughts.

Controlling and managing your thoughts is one of the basic tenants of Zen Buddhism, for example. In the Christian context, the apostle Paul said, "Be transformed by the renewing of your mind." Philosophers, educators, and thinkers of every generation conclude the same thing.

> *Change your thoughts, and you can change your feelings. Change your emotions, and you can change your behavior. Change your behavior and you can change your results.*

But the power of this truth is not reserved just for philosophers. Salespeople can make use of it as well.

The reason you may feel depressed or anxious is because you are thinking depressing or anxious thoughts. Change your thoughts, and you can change your feelings. Change your emotions, and you can change your behavior. Change your behavior and you can change your results.

It's not as difficult as it may sound.

Do this — invest in a couple of audio programs – good, positive stuff like my *Smart Selling*, or *How to Become a Master of Distributor Sales*. Or, find something at the local library. Then, as you drive between appointments, and on your way home after work, listen to those tapes or CDs. You'll find yourself thinking positive thoughts. Those positive thoughts will lead to a more positive attitude. That attitude will evidence itself in more focused actions. Those actions will lead to better results.

Read educational and inspiring books and periodicals. There are literally hundreds of good sales books published each year. Spend 30 minutes at your local Barnes & Noble, Borders or business book store and you'll find several works that will interest and stimulate you.

The World Wide Web is awash with resources. In addition to my own monthly Ezine, I'm aware of at least five regular electronic publications for salespeople, and there are probably dozens more.

Then there are hardcopy publications. Check out *Selling Power* and *Sales & Marketing Management* – two classy professional publications. I'm on the editorial advisory panels of three paper publications – newsletters that will serve to stimulate and encourage you. There are, of course, dozens of others.

There is no realistic limit to the amount of positive, educational material available to you. If you are not regularly exposing yourself to some of this, it is because you are choosing to not be motivated. If nothing else, sign up for my free monthly Ezine at www.davekahle.com.

All of these sources will give you ideas, stimulate your mind and encourage you. The result will be more positive thoughts. And the result of that will be a motivated, successful person.

Succeeding in difficult times requires you to take charge of your motivation.

Now is the time to take this most important step to becoming a true professional.

Q #28. *I find it difficult to stay upbeat and positive all the time. I have a tendency to get down on myself when something goes poorly and then find it hard to look forward to the next sales call. I can't be the only salesperson who struggles with this. Can you help?*

A. Thanks for asking a question that the vast majority of salespeople don't have the courage to ask. Yep, the situation you described is an occupational hazard. Most salespeople have times when they are hesitant to make the next call or take the next step because they've just been rejected in the last.

I think that salespeople, in particular, are sensitive to this. Two reasons – first, we face rejection more times in the course of a week than almost any other job title. Second, since we spend so much time alone, we often mentally dwell on our shortcomings and failures much more than the person who works in an office or in proximity to other people.

So much for the problem. Are there any solutions? Of course.

For now, let me focus on just one. About ten years ago, Martin Seligman, PhD., authored a book called *Learned Optimism*. I expect that it is out of print, but if you can find a copy I'd recommend that you do so. *Learned Optimism* provides a solid answer to your challenge.

In it, Seligman describes his lifework. As a research psychologist, Dr. Seligman began by studying helplessness in dogs. In an early experiment, he put dogs into a cage from which they could not escape, and subjected them to mild shocks. After some effort at escape, the dogs would give up trying and lay down. Later, he put them into a cage from which they could easily escape, and subjected them to the same mild shocks. The dogs would just lie down and give up. Surprisingly, they did not attempt to remove themselves from the irritant. They had learned helplessness and hopelessness.

In subsequent experiments, Dr. Seligman found a similar behavior in human beings. Put into a room and subjected to irritating noises from which they could not escape, they soon learned to give up. When put into a room with a mechanism that would turn off the noise, they still didn't try. They had learned helplessness and hopelessness.

From this beginning, Dr. Seligman continued to formulate a theory he calls "learned optimism." It says, basically, that human beings learn to have either a pessimistic or an optimistic outlook. Dr. Seligman's book contains a self-assessment to measure the degree of pessimism or optimism of the reader.

Dr. Seligman's theory arises from the way people explain negative events to themselves. When something negative happens, as it eventually will, the way you explain it to yourself determines your pessimistic/optimistic attitude. There are three components of this "explanatory style."

The first component is the degree to which you believe the event will be *permanent*. Pessimists believe negative events will be permanent, while optimists believe that they will be temporary.

The second component is *pervasiveness*. Pessimists believe the causes of negative events are universal, affecting everything they do. Optimists believe them to be specific, and limited to the individual circumstances.

The third component is *personal*. Pessimists believe that negative events are caused by themselves. Optimists believe that the world is at fault.

Here's how this behavioral perspective works in the everyday life of a salesperson.

Let's say you visit one of your large accounts, and your main contact announces that the vice-president for operations has signed a prime vendor agreement with your largest competitor, and that all of your business will be moved to that competitor within the next 30 days. *That's* a negative event.

As you drive away from the account, you think to yourself, "I blew it here. I should have seen it coming. I'm never going to learn this job. I'll blow the next one too. I mismanage them all."

Now, that's a pessimistic explanation of the event. Notice that you have explained it in a way that is personal, "*I* blew it." Your explanation is also permanent, "I'm *never* going to learn to do this job," and pervasive, "I mismanage them *all*."

Now stop a minute, and analyze how you feel as a result of this explanation. Probably defeated, dejected, depressed, and passive. These are not the kinds of feelings you need to energize you to make your next sales call.

Let's revisit the situation, this time offering optimistic explanations. The same event occurs – you receive bad news from your best account. As you drive away, you think to yourself, "They really made a bad mistake this time. It's a good thing the contract is only for a year. That gives me time to work to get it back. I'm glad it was only this account and no others."

That's an optimistic explanation because your explanations were not personal, permanent, or pervasive. How do you feel about your future as a result of this explanation? Probably energized and hopeful.

See the difference? The event was the same. The only difference was the way you explained it to yourself. One set of explanations was optimistic, leading to energy and hope, while the other was pessimistic, leading to dejection and passivity.

Dr. Seligman has isolated optimistic behavior as one of the characteristics of successful people. Using various techniques he's developed, he predicted elections by analyzing each candidate's explanatory style. The most optimistic candidates often win elections.

The implications for you are awesome. If you can improve your explanatory style, and make it more optimistic, you'll create more positive energy and hope for yourself, no matter how difficult or negative the circumstances with which you must deal.

Learned optimism can be one of your most powerful self-management techniques.

It's based on this powerful principle:

Your thoughts influence your feelings and your actions, and you can choose your thoughts. Here's how he suggests that you do that.

Step One. Analyze your explanatory habits.

Wait until you must deal with some negative event or some adversity in your life. Then, stop and observe what you are telling yourself about the event. What do you believe about yourself and the reason why bad things happen? Ask to what degree your explanations are personal, permanent or pervasive?

Step Two. Note the consequences of your explanatory style.

Pessimistic explanations always lead to passivity and dejection. Optimistic explanations always lead to energy and hope. Which is more likely to propel you to future success?

Step Three. If you're pessimistic, you must change the way you think.

Your future success depends on your ability to rise up and meet adversity with renewed energy and optimism. You can do this by choosing to think differently. Dr. Seligman makes the following suggestions.

Distract your thoughts. In other words, when you find yourself thinking negative and pessimistic thoughts, tell yourself to "Stop!" You can even say it out loud, or shout it to yourself. Just "STOP" thinking those things.

Then, shift your thoughts to something else. I'd suggest you think about something that brings you pleasure or satisfaction, or something at which you're good.

Dispute your explanations. This is a longer-lasting approach. Argue with yourself. Reason your way out of your negative thoughts. Look at the evidence, or suggest alternatives. Reason from the implications or usefulness of what you're thinking.

Back to our example. On the way out to your car after your miserable call, you are thinking to yourself "I blew it here. I should have seen it coming. I'm never going to learn this job. I'll blow the next one, too. I mismanage them all."

When you catch yourself thinking defeating thoughts, argue with yourself. Think, "Wait a minute. While it's true I may have been able to do something if I had seen this coming, the truth is that the VP would never see me. The other company must have had some special "in". That doesn't mean that this will work anywhere else. It's just this account. There certainly isn't any evidence of this possibility happening anywhere else. And, the truth is that the entire purchasing department is not happy about this course of events. If I stay close to the account, they may find lots of reasons to continue to do business with me."

What you've done is argue with yourself in order to change your thought processes. As a result of thinking differently, you have more energy, more hope and, therefore, more likelihood of success in the future.

You can change your thoughts. You can choose to think differently. You can choose to believe differently.

And that fundamental decision about how you think can, more than any other single decision, affect your future success.

Dr. Seligman has discovered, through his scientific research, a truth that has been known for thousands of years. The Apostle Paul, writing in the book of Romans, counseled new Christians to "Be transformed by the renewing of your mind." And Solomon said that "As a man thinks in his heart, so is he."

Your choice of what to think about, and how to think about what happens to you, is one of the most important choices you'll ever make.

So, when you find yourself feeling depressed, dejected and with little energy, recognize how you are thinking, and think differently.

13

PENETRATING THE IMPENETRABLE ACCOUNT

The Impenetrable Account

How do I sell to an account that is firmly in the hands of a competitor?

In one form or another, I hear that question at almost every sales seminar I teach. It's a great question, reflecting one of the most perplexing and frustrating situations every salesperson faces. If you haven't yet been faced with this problem, be patient, you will be soon.

Here's how this usually develops: You've called on a high-potential account a number of times, but can't seem to get anywhere. The more time you spend in the account, the more apparent it is that one or more of your competitors is deeply ingrained as suppliers to that account. You may even have had someone say to you, "We do all our business with XYZ competitor."

And that leaves you on the outside looking in. If the account has some real potential, you want to be seriously considered as a supplier. But it looks like this account is not really interested in you – not because of you or your company, but because of a previously established, strong relationship with a competitor.

So, how do you manage this account? What should you do?

Let's start with what not to do.

Don't vent your frustration by speaking poorly about the competition. And don't attack the competitor's products, company, practices or salespeople. Someone who works for this customer – or more likely, several people who work there – chose to do business with that competitor. They have chosen to buy the competitor's products, have developed a close working relationship, and may be good friends outside of work. When you speak badly about the competition, you insult all those decisions made by the customer to work with that particular competitor. Trying to penetrate an account by insulting your customer's judgement is not a particularly effective technique.

Realize, also, that you have only a tiny glimpse of what your competitor is really like. You may have found some evidence in another account of their ineptness, or what you perceive as unethical behavior. And on the basis of this tiny experience, you're ready to launch a holy crusade to reveal their deep flaws and expose the risks of doing business with them.

That is almost never the truth. Almost always, your competitor is a company with the products, ethics, business systems, people and goals that are very similar to yours. Very few companies survive in this highly competitive marketplace if they have shoddy products, lax business morals, incompetent people, and poor operating systems. When you criticize these things in your competitor, you show yourself to be ignorant and inexperienced.

But what should you do?

Here are two proven techniques to penetrate these kinds of accounts.

1. Go around the competition, not through them.

This customer is probably not buying *everything* from your primary competitor. There likely is a handful of other suppliers selling items that you could supply. Focus on those. Find items that are being purchased from someone other than the main vendor, and present your company's options on those. Often these could be small quantities of relatively inconspicuous items that don't appear on the radar screen of your competitor.

When you put together attractive programs and proposals for those kinds of items, you don't threaten your customer's relationship with your competitor, and you begin to show them the value of a relationship with you.

Be careful to keep a relatively low profile in the account. You don't want to draw your competitor's attention. At first, as you try to pick off some of these miscellaneous items, you are very vulnerable to your primary competitor finding and squashing you. As time goes by and you're successful at becoming the supplier of a number of miscellaneous items, you'll gain power and position within the account, and in so doing, build some defenses against the ire of your competitor. You're always safer if your competitor underestimates your activity and success within an account. So, at least until you're well established, be as discreet and inconspicuous as possible.

Here's a number of ways to implement this strategy of "going around the competition."

A. Find some area within the customer's business where the competition is very weak. For example, when I was selling hospital supplies, I discovered that one of my major competitors was very strong in the operating room. The competitor had a wide range of products, well-respected lines, a history of being active and interested in that area of the hospital, and significant expertise in operating room procedures and problems. So, I didn't bother with the operating room, and spent my time in respiratory therapy and ICU. The competition never bothered to visit those departments. I went around my competition by finding a department on which to focus where the competition was weak.

B. Find someone who doesn't like dealing with your competitor. This may take longer. In a large organization, there are often dozens of decision-makers and influencers. It's likely that one or more of them may not like dealing with your competitor. Maybe personalities clashed sometime in the past, or someone felt slighted or rudely treated. Regardless, someone inside that organization may not be your competitor's biggest fan. Find that person(s).

But don't be too quick to bet your future on that relationship. Before you begin to work with that person, access that person's political power within the account. It may be that the champion you selected is viewed as a perpetual complainer who never has any constructive opinions to offer. If that's the case, you'll hurt yourself in the account by aligning with him/her.

If you come to the conclusion that your champion is a strong and respected player within the account, then focus on building a relationship and equipping that person to pursue his or her own agenda with your assistance.

Here's the second major strategy for penetrating the impenetrable account.

2. Make a persistent, strong appeal to be the secondary supplier for that account.

Here's one important thing you know about this customer: They are loyal to their key supplier. That indicates a philosophical position this customer holds – these are people who believe in loyalty to suppliers who do a good job in their account. That's why they continue to buy from your competitor.

So, use that position to your own advantage. Make a consistent appeal to the customer that they ought to have the same kind of relationship with a back-up supplier – you. You're not implying criticism of the primary supplier, but things that are out of their control can happen, and the continuity of supplies can be interrupted. In that case, it's to the customer's advantage to have a good relationship with a secondary supplier. That's an argument that often resonates effectively within this kind of account. If they agree with that position, then it follows that they need to be doing some business with you in order to keep you interested and active within the account. And that should lead to a discussion of what you can be selling to them.

> *Your job is to stay in front of the customer and position yourself to be the customer's easiest, lowest risk choice when things finally do change with the competition.*

Both of these strategies require you to be persistent in visiting the account and staying visible to them, even in the face of little success or encouragement from them. Assuming that the potential of the account is worth the investment, this persistency may be your key strategy.

I was faced with this exact situation on more than one occasion. As I was venting my frustration over a particularly difficult account, my manager counseled me like this: "The only thing you can count on," he said, " is that things will change. We don't know how, and we don't know when, but we do know that things will change. Your job is to stay in front of the customer and position yourself to be the customer's easiest, lowest risk choice when things finally do change with the competition."

What great advice that turned out to be. The best example was a medium-sized account not far from my home. On my first call there, I met with the head of purchasing. After listening politely to my presentation, he said, "Young man, we already have too many vendors. We don't want to add new ones; we want to eliminate some we already have. Secondly, we don't know much about your company, but what we do know we don't like. So, I'd advise you not to waste your time here."

I considered that a real challenge.

So, about six weeks later, I returned with my strongest product. This was a product called suction tubing, which is a staple item in a hospital. Every hospital uses it in all sorts of ways and places throughout their operations. We had an exclusive with the country's largest and best manufacturer of suction tubing, coupled with excellent pricing. He couldn't say no to my deal on suction tubing.

Again, he listened patiently to my presentation. When I had finished, he said, "We don't use any." I looked through the open door of his office, and saw a supply cart in the hall outside, with suction tubing hanging from it. He was lying to me. I knew it, and he knew that I knew it.

"This really is going to be a challenge," I thought to myself. As I reflected on the account, it became apparent that he was protecting a relationship with my arch competitor. I decided on two lines of attack: Find someone to sell to who wasn't enamored with the competitor, and hang in there as an easy choice if, and when, the competitor stumbled.

That's exactly what happened. I found one of the purchasing agents who was interested in what my company had to offer. When the competitor was backordered on an item, the customer turned to us. We were able to deliver. That eventually lead to us obtaining the contract for that item. And that opened the door, gave me a foothold in the account, and allowed me an opportunity to begin working within it.

Three years later, that account had become one of my best. I had penetrated it to a greater degree than any others. And, the head of purchasing that had previously so ardently protected the relationship with my competitor, now just as ardently protected the relationship with me.

That is what makes it all worthwhile. Almost always, those accounts that protect a relationship with your competitor will just as fervently protect the relationship with you when you become their primary supplier. The payoff is well worth the investment.

Q #29. *"How can I sell more when I have so much to do?"*

A. That's a question I'm often asked whenever I'm talking to a group of salespeople. I'm sure you can empathize with the feelings behind it. You have new products to learn, paperwork to complete, hundreds of customer problems to solve, meetings to attend, inside people to cajole, managers to mollify – and on top of all this, you are expected to sell something!

It's hard to do so when you have all these other aspects of your job howling for your attention.

How do you manage all of this while at the same time you build your sales? How do you sort through all of this and focus on the essentials of your job?

Good question. Let's start by identifying one of those essentials. Think about the sales process – the activities that it takes to make a sale – and certain key activities come to mind. You know that you need to make appointments with qualified decision makers, to collect information about their needs, to build relationships, to demonstrate products, to follow up, to answer questions, etc. Your list of important sales activities is probably expanding monthly. But if you're going to focus on the essentials, there is one absolutely necessary activity around which everything else revolves. All of the other activities are either means to bring about this activity, or actions that spring out of this one key activity.

What is it? *Making a persuasive offer to your customer.* Think of it as an **offer.** In its simplest terms, making an *offer* means saying something like this to your customer, "Here is this... (product, service, package, deal, etc.). How about buying it?"

You make an *offer* whenever you respond to a request for a price. When you demonstrate a product, you make an *offer*. When you bring in a piece of literature and tell your customer about some new product or service, you make an *offer*. When you respond to your customer's request with information about a product or service, you make an *offer*. All of these are variations on a theme, but all of them can be classified as the presentation of an *offer*.

And those *offers* are the heart of your job. Without them, you can sell nothing. Your customers will never buy if you never *offer* them something to buy.

It is an unmistakable fact of life that in sales, quantity counts. In other words, to be successful, you must make a certain quantity of sales *offers*. No matter how much skill and sophistication you apply to your job as a salesperson, you cannot totally negate the quantity aspect of it. Given two salespeople in approximately equal territories, or of approximately equal abilities, the one who makes the greater quantity of sales *offers* will generally have better results than the other salesperson.

With this in mind, one simple way to cut through all the mass of things that you have to do is to focus on the essential component of the sales process – making an appropriate quantity of sales *offers*. If you're looking for a simple way to increase your results, focus on the quantity of sales offers that you make.

Do two things. First, begin to keep track of how many of these sales *offers* you make in the course of a week. Initially, don't worry about what you're presenting, and don't be concerned about the dollar volume of each potential piece of business. Those are more sophisticated concerns that can be considered later. For now, just keep track of how many *offers* you make. Use a simple hash mark system in your planner. Each day, make a hash mark for each *offer* you presented to a customer. At the end of each week, add up the number of hash marks.

There is an amazing law of management that states that the behavior that you measure is the behavior that you get. That applies to self-management as well. Just the act of keeping track (measuring) the quantity of sales *offers* you present will help you to focus on those essential activities. As you become more aware of the quantity of sales *offers*, you'll naturally be drawn to ways to increase that quantity.

Which brings me to the second thing you need to do. Begin to find ways to increase the quantity of those sales *offers*. If you find yourself averaging five presentations a week, try to increase that to an average of ten.

When I was a new distributor salesperson, my manager told me that I ought to attempt to have at least one new product to present at every sales call. I thought he probably knew better than I did, so I did what he suggested. At some point along the way, I began to think in terms of the quantity of sales *offers*. It occurred to me that I could double the number of sales *offers* I made by taking two or more products in to every sales call. So I began to spend a little more time preparing my samples and literature each week, so that I could dramatically increase the quantity of sales *offers* I made. That simple strategy was certainly part of my one million dollar a year increase in sales.

It can be for you, too. When you're overwhelmed with too much to do, and when you're feeling like you're being drawn into a kaleidoscope of conflicting directions, focus on the essential part of your job. Measure and increase the quantity of sales *offers* you make. It will keep you close to the heart of your job and help you focus on the highest priority activities.

Q #30. I am dealing with a particular dilemma with which I have yet to become comfortable. I am having trouble coming to terms with constantly calling on customers and potential customers who are not buying. Some say they will call when they need something, and some say that they have no need for my products and services. I am having trouble figuring out how to approach the businesses without becoming a nuisance, and how to justify my presence when they have not contacted me for assistance. I am in search of an approach that I can feel comfortable and respectable about, without sacrificing potential orders.

A. I have a number of suggestions for you. First, let's create some realistic expectations. You are always going to be challenged by this situation. It comes with the territory, and is part of almost every salesperson's challenge. There is no magic bullet, nor 25 word pitch that guarantees your customers will suddenly become open and receptive. Instead, there are some techniques that have proven to be effective. Your job is to pick those that seem most appropriate for each customer.

Having said that, my first thought has to do with your comment that some say they have no need for your products and services. Are you qualifying the customer before you call on them? Are you researching them, and coming to the conclusion that they really do need or could benefit from what you sell? If not, that may account for some of the difficulty in some accounts. If they really, truly have no need or interest in what you are selling, you should not be calling on them. So, step one, make sure you are doing a good job of qualifying the customer before you call on them.

If you are able to see them, try to demonstrate your competence by asking a few questions about their applications that they may never have heard before. That gets them thinking, and positions you as someone who is an expert in their product. Try to get a plant or facility tour, and look for problems or opportunities which your product(s) could impact.

Or, every time you see them, try to bring some piece of information or insight that will help them — perhaps the details of a new product or a new application of something they are currently using. If you can establish yourself as someone who brings them useful information, you'll eventually earn a consistent audience.

Or, try making an outright appeal to be number two. They probably have a current supplier with whom they are happy. Don't threaten that relationship, and don't bad mouth that supplier, just appeal to be their back up supplier in the case of some change in, or problem with, their current supplier. That gives you a reason to be there, and gives them a reason to find out what you have.

If you are not able to see them, consider asking one of your current customers to recommend or introduce you.

Or, make it a point to try to meet them in a situation outside of their business. Look them up at trade shows, or association meetings.

Finally, sometimes the issue is timing. It's not that they are not interested, it's just that they are too busy at the moment when you happen to be there. Try calling at different times of the day or different days of the week. You may strike them at a time when it's more relaxed and more convenient for them to talk to you.

RESOURCES AVAILABLE FROM THE DACO CORPORATION

Because we specialize in helping distributors and the manufacturers who sell through them to increase their sales and develop their people, we have created a number of resources to assist you. For the latest resources and prices, visit our website at www.davekahle.com.

1. Books:

How to Excel at Distributor Sales

This classic book provides a written reminder of the material in the training session, and can be used individually as well as the subject for small group discussions. For more information, visit www.nawpubs.org.

Take Your Sales Performance Up-a-Notch

Another classic which is available in four languages and 20 countries. Visit www.davekahle.com/upnotch.htm.

Ten Secrets of Time Management for Salespeople

The most recent book is an easy read with powerful strategies and tools to make every minute count. Visit www.davekahle.com/10secrets.htm.

Transforming Your Sales Force for the 21st Century

Written for the Chief Sales Officer, this book spells out the ten most effective initiatives most distributors can take to jump start their sales systems. Visit www.davekahle.com/transforming.htm.

2. TGIF & K monthly phone seminars:

These monthly phone seminars focus on developing sales mastery. **TGIF & K**... stands for *"Thank Goodness It's Friday and Kahle."* A new topic is developed every month, and each program is one hour, on one Friday every month. Each program is crafted to inspire, educate and motivate your sales staff! Visit www.davekahle.com/virtual.htm.

3. To assist in the hiring of new salespeople, our pre-hire aptititude assessments:

Why go through the hassle of long, extensive interviews when you have an assessment tool that can slice through the digging and prodding that goes into "knowing" the applicant? Our Sales Aptitude Identifier is a sophisticated benchmark that can prevent many time-wasting interviews. With this computerized pre-hire sales assessment, you'll take the guesswork out of hiring a good salesperson and improve your chances of making a profitable hire. Visit www.davekahle.com/profiles/salesindicator.htm.

Our pre-hire assessments are available for:

- Inside Sales
- Customer Service Representatives
- Service Sales (Business-to-Business)
- Distributor Sales of Capital Equipment
- Distributor Sales of Consumable Products
- Manufacturers Selling through Distributors

4. To assist in the training and development of new salespeople: "First Steps to Success in Outside Sales"

This CD ROM, self-study program establishes the habits necessary for success in the new distributor salesperson, reducing the time it takes to make him/her profitable. Visit www.davekahle.com/firststeps.htm.

5. How to Become a Master of Distributor Sales

Another CD ROM, self-study program that is designed to bring the experienced salesperson to a higher level of competence and confidence. Visit www.davekahle.com/master.htm.

6. The Kahle Way® Distributor Selling System

We customize our ultimate selling system to the specifics of your environment, and teach your salespeople the program in a two-day, interactive seminar followed by regular reinforcement sessions. We bring this to your company, and offer two annual public training sessions every year. Visit www.davekahle.com/distributorsalespeople.htm.

7. The Kahle Way® Distributor Sales Management System

The ultimate solution for helping a sales/branch manager take his sales force to higher levels of performance and accountability. Visit www.davekahle.com/distributorselling system.htm.

8. Top Gun Seminars for Distributor Salespeople

Every fall we produce a series of one-day seminars and bring them to locations around the country. Top Gun Seminars are designed to inspire and educate distributor salespeople with the strategies and practices that will ensure their ability to survive and prosper. Visit www.davekahle.com/topgun/seminar.htm.

9. Live, customized presentations and seminars by Dave Kahle

Dave is one of the premier sales speakers in the country. He's a world class speaker who has presented in 43 states and six countries. Bring Dave in to motivate, educate and inspire your sales force.

ABOUT THE AUTHOR...

Dave Kahle is a consultant and speaker who specializes in helping distributors and their suppliers grow their sales and develop their people. He's a world-class speaker who has presented in six countries and 43 states.

He has acquired his message through real-life experience. As a distributor salesperson, Dave took a new territory to over $5,000,000 in sales in 5 short years, becoming the top sales person in the nation. He's been the number one salesperson in the country for two different companies in two separate industries.

As a general manager of a start-up division of a distribution company, Dave directed that company's growth from $10,000 in monthly sales to over $200,000 in just 38 months.

*Since 1988, he's served as president of the DaCo Corporation. Dave has trained thousands of salespeople, and has authored six books, 32 multi-media programs, and has been published over 500 times. His credits include: **How to Excel at Distributor Sales, Take Your Sales Performance Up-A-Notch, 10 Secrets of Time Management for Salespeople** and his latest book, **Transforming Your Sales Force For The 21st Century.***

Dave serves on the editorial panel of The Competitive Edge and is a contributing editor to Sales & Marketing Excellence newsletter.

He holds a Bachelor of Arts degree from the University of Toledo, and a Master's degree from Bowling Green State University. He and his wife live in Grand Rapids, MI, where he is a father, a step-father, an adoptive father, a foster father, and a grandfather.

Dave is a member of the Author's Guild, the Christian Businessmen's Committee, and the American Society for Training and Development.

He can be reached at:

The DaCo Corporation
P.O. Box 230017
Grand Rapids, MI 49503
(800) 331-1287 toll free
(616) 451-9377 phone
(616) 451-9412 facsimile
info@davekahle.com
www.DaveKahle.com